MEN *of the* PROMISE

BECOMING A MAN OF COURAGEOUS FAITH

ED HINDSON

HARVEST HOUSE
PUBLISHERS
EUGENE, OREGON 97402

MEN OF THE PROMISE

Copyright ©1996 by Harvest House Publishers
Eugene, Oregon 97402

Library of Congress Cataloging-in-Publication Data

Hindson, Edward E.
    Men of the promise / Ed Hindson.
        p. cm.
    ISBN 1–56507–513–7
    1. Men–Religious life.   2. Men (Christian theology)   3. Men in the Bible–Meditations.
    4. Bible. O.T.–Meditations.   I. Title.
    BV4528.2.H56   1996
    248.8'42–dc20   96-22672
                                                                                          CIP

Printed in the United States of America.

96 97 98 99 00 01 02 /BC/ 10 9 8 7 6 5 4 3 2 1

*To Donna
my wonderful wife
on our 30th anniversary.*

Contents

Preface:

Becoming Men of the Promise

Promises! Promises! The fabric which hopes and dreams are made of. Promises encourage our hearts and lift our souls. They keep us going when the going gets tough. They also express the deepest commitments of our lives. And they remind us of the greatest promise of all—God's promise—which transforms ordinary men into men of God.

The promise is an expression of the divine Promisor. It is His commitment to extend His grace and power to all those who will trust in Him. The Bible calls it His "holy promise" (Psalm 105:42). And it calls those who believe in it "children of promise" (Galatians 4:28).

This book is a study of that promise and the lives of the men it transforms. It is the incredible story of dynamic encounters with the power of God. Power that transformed ordinary men into men of God. Walk with them through the pages of Scripture. Experience God at work in their lives. And discover Him at work in your life as well.

This study focuses on the lives of the "Hebrew heroes" from the Old Testament. Each one of them met God personally, believed His promises, and was changed forever by an encounter with the Promisor.

Over the past 20 years, I have taught the Old Testament to more than 20,000 college and university students. My goal has always been to make the Old Testament come alive to them. I want them to see these biblical characters as real men. Men with hopes and dreams. Men with successes and failures. Men with ups and downs. Men with good times and bad times. But always as men of the promise. Men who held onto truth and never let go. Men who found God to be the ultimate reality of life itself.

During the past several years, I have also had the wonderful opportunity to share the lives of these great men of God with a thousand men who have attended our *Atlanta Men for Christ* weekly businessmen's luncheons. What a thrill it has been to see their lives challenged by these great truths. And what a joy to see these men growing in the grace of God and in the power of His Spirit.

Each one of us has much to learn. The longer you live, the more you will realize that life is a journey of faith. Martin Luther once said of this journey, "We are not yet what we shall be but we are growing toward it. The process is not yet finished but is going on. This is not the end but it is the road." Walk with me back in time as we join these great men of God on the road to glory.

I especially want to thank my wife, Donna, for her love, encouragement, and patience. And my daughter, Christy Hindson Murphy, for her editorial assistance. My thanks also to Mrs. Emily Boothe, my administrative assistant, whose devotion and persistence saw this project through to completion. May God be glorified!

He keeps His promises!

The Promise

His divine power has given us everything we need for life and godliness. . . . Through these he has given us his very great and precious promises, so that through them you may participate in the divine nature and escape the corruption in the world caused by evil desires.

–2 Peter 1:3,4

Introduction:

It Begins in the Heart of the Promisor

The promise has always been there from the very beginning. It was born in the heart of God and grows in the hearts of men of faith. As real as the air we breathe and lives we live. It is the most powerful force on earth. Because it's the demonstration of the most powerful Person in the universe—the divine Promisor.

It began in eternity past. When God foresaw the mess we men would make of things. It was then that He decided to do something to correct it all. It was then that the promise began. And it echoed through the Garden of Eden where Paradise was lost. "Your offspring will crush the head of the serpent," God promised. And the process began for the promise to be fulfilled.

When men turned their backs on God, He responded in judgment. And the flood swept them all away. But Noah found grace and was spared. After that, the promise came in the form of a "covenant"—an agreement between God and man. "I now establish my covenant with you and with your descendants after you" (Genesis 9:9), God told Noah and all mankind.

But men still rebelled. More judgment followed. And men were scattered all over the face of the earth. That's when God began His regathering process. Since multitudes of men turned away from Him, God turned away from them. It was then, in about 2100 B.C., that He turned to one man—Abraham—to keep the promise alive.

God called Abraham to follow Him to a land He promised to give to him and his descendants—the land of Canaan. It was there that God made a covenant with Abraham (see Genesis 15:18). The promise was personalized to one man out of the entire human race. Later, it would be confirmed to others: Isaac, Jacob, Judah, and David. In fact, the promise would become the theme of the Old Testament Hebrew Scriptures. Old Testament scholar Dr. Walter Kaiser calls the promise the "theological center" of the Hebrew Bible.

As time passed, God made it clear that the people of Israel were the people of the promise. And that the land of Israel was the place of the promise. And that David and the line of Davidic kings were the kings of the promise. Finally, the Old Testament prophets foresaw the coming Messiah as the ultimate fulfillment of the promise. As Gentile powers marched across the scenes of human history, the people of Israel never lost sight of the Promised One. They kept waiting. Hoping. Expecting Him to come.

When Jesus did come, He announced: "Do you think that I have come to abolish the Law or the Prophets; I have not come to abolish them but to fulfill them" (Matthew 5:17). And fulfill them He did! With such magnitude that He exceeded the greatest expectations of those whose hopes had held out so long.

In Jesus, the promise took on flesh and blood. It was incarnate in the Savior Himself. Thus, the new form of the promise, the new covenant, superseded the old covenant. The writer of Hebrews puts it like this: "But the ministry Jesus has received is as superior to theirs as the covenant of which he is mediator is superior to the old one, and it is founded on better promises" (8:6).

Better promises! Better because He is the fulfillment of the promise. Without Him there is no completion. But with Him, all things are complete. Hebrews 11 lists the great Hebrew heroes of the Old Testament: Noah, Abraham, Isaac, Jacob, Joseph, Moses, Joshua, Gideon, Samson, Jephthah, David, Daniel. And then, verses 39 and 40 add: "These were all commended for their faith, yet none of them received what had been promised. God had planned something better for us so that only together with us would they be made perfect."

The promise was there all the time. It kept them going when times were tough. It was always just ahead. Over the next horizon. That means these Old Testament believers kept pursuing it, but never saw it fully realized until Jesus came. But when He came, all their hopes and dreams were complete.

When the aged Simeon held the infant Jesus at the Temple, he announced:

> Sovereign Lord, as you have promised, you now dismiss your servant in peace. For my eyes have seen your salvation, which you have prepared in the sight of all people (Luke 2:29,30).

The Promisor had come in human flesh. A baby's cry broke the silence of the centuries between the testaments. And in that infant's cry, the turning point of human history came. The promise had been fulfilled. The Savior had come to redeem us from the curse of sin. Divine hope lit up the night. The Light of the world had come, and things would never be the same. The Promisor had kept the promise!

CHAPTER

1

Getting Started:

The Journey of Faith

Beginnings are exciting! They are the starting points of a brand-new life. Each new step·has challenges and opportunities of its own. But that first step really takes a lot of faith. Remember the first time you drove a car? Asked a girl for a date? Started college? Took a job? Asked a woman to marry you? Held your first child?

Each new step is an adventure. It requires taking a risk. It is a step of faith—an act of trust by which we commit ourselves to someone or something. Faith is believing. Believing in the object of our trust. Believing in ourselves. Believing in another person. Ultimately, believing in God.

Faith is so important that it is mentioned over 300 times in the Bible. The first reference to believing in God is found in the story of Abraham. The Scripture says, "Abram believed the LORD, and he credited it to him as righteousness" (Genesis 15:6). This particular step of faith is so important that the above statement is repeated again three times in the New Testament (Romans 4:3; Galatians 3:6; James 2:23).

The power of our faith rests in the object of our faith. At the foundation of all love is a belief in the object that is loved. If I do not believe in a person, I cannot love him. The same is true in our relationship with God. Without faith it is impossible for us to know Him or love Him. Faith is the starting point in our spiritual journey. We must begin with God: believing that He exists, believing that He cares, and believing that His love is real.

For Abraham, the starting point came 4000 years ago (c. 2100 B.C.) in a burgeoning metropolis near the Persian Gulf. At the time, he was wealthy, successful, and prosperous. The last thing he needed to do was to abandon everything and follow God. That's where the Promise comes in. It was born in the heart of God in eternity past. Yet it still expresses itself in the extension of His grace in our lives.

The Bible expresses it like this:

> The Lord had said to Abram, "Leave your country, your people and your father's household and go to the land I will show you. I will make you into a great nation and I will bless you; I will make your name great, and you will be a blessing!" (Genesis 12:1,2).

God asked Abraham to leave everything that was near and dear to him to go to the land that He would show him. Abraham had no idea where it was. All he knew was that God promised to bless him and make him into a great nation.

However, there was a problem with all this—his name. In Hebrew, *Abram* means "great father." But he didn't have any children! So his name became a constant source of frustration to him. We can just imagine every time he met someone...

> "Hi, what's your name?"
> "Great father."

"Really. How many kids do you have?"
"None!"

His name didn't fit his circumstances. And in those days, that was a real problem because names were given based on their meaning and significance. But God knew that all along. That's why He promised to make a "great nation" of him. It was God's way of personalizing His promises. He was telling Abram that things were going to change, and they were going to change dramatically.

The Ultimate Change Agent

God is the ultimate change agent. The world He created is constantly changing. People themselves are in a continual process of change. Living organisms are not static; they are constantly changing. Change comes when we are willing to grow and improve. Change involves several key elements:

1. *Honest view of the past.* You won't change as long as you are satisfied with the way things are. Such attitudes may make us content for a while, but they can also leave us unwilling to change when we really need to change.

2. *Dissatisfaction with the present.* There is something wholesome in a holy dissatisfaction with the status quo. Good leaders are always asking how they can improve and make things better. Unless we begin asking the tough questions now, we may wait too long to take action.

3. *Hope for the future.* Great leaders are always optimistic about the future. They embrace it and make the most of it. They realize that change is a necessary part of personal improvement.

Larry and Rosalie Lefler are dear friends of ours. Larry owns a business supplies company in St. Louis. Several years ago, Larry invited me to have lunch with him to discuss making some important changes in his life. He was going through a time of serious reflection and a general reevaluation of his goals and priorities.

After we settled down to eat, I realized Larry really wanted to talk seriously about his life, his family, and his future. Larry is a kind and sensitive person who really takes advice to heart. As we talked about his personal growth and development, I reminded him that pride is the key element we have to overcome in making changes in our lives. Most of us are too proud to admit we need to change.

The Little Piece of Paper

I took out a small piece of note paper and wrote out a series of simple instructions about narrowing our options from our general interests to our abilities, limitations, gifts, motivations, and opportunities. I drew a chart that looked something like this:

I explained to Larry that God creates each one of us with certain interests, abilities, limitations, motivations, and gifts. These vary from person to person. But ours are unique to us. They are the "stuff" from which our God-given potential is made. God takes our *potential* and, as we refine, develop, and accept our general interests, abilities, limitations, motivations, and spiritual gifts, we clarify our options in pursuit of our God-given *opportunities* in life.

The rest is a matter of *choice.* We must choose which options we will take in pursuit of those opportunities God sets before us. As we make those choices, we must do so in light of certain biblical priorities regarding our relationship to God, marriage, family, church, business, and community. Something clicked inside Larry's heart. The timing was right for him to make some serious changes in his life at that moment. God spoke to him clearly and powerfully during that luncheon. Afterward, Larry asked if he could keep the little scrap of paper. He put it into his wallet and thanked me for my advice. It was several years later that I learned that he continued to keep that paper in his wallet. He looked at it almost daily as he sought God's will for his life over the next several months.

When we were preparing to move to Atlanta from St. Louis, Larry took me out to lunch to thank me for all our friendship had meant to him. It was one of those emotionally moving experiences that bond two men together. In the course of the lunch, he mentioned the conversation we had years earlier. Then he pulled out his wallet and showed me the scrap of paper I had written on previously.

"I have kept it all this time," he said with tears in his eyes. "You will never know how much that little piece of paper has helped me over the years. God began a change in my heart that day that is still going on today. It is a spiritual journey, and I love every step of it!"

Taking That First Step

Abram said yes to God's call, and he stepped out by faith on a spiritual journey that would change the course of history. He gathered up his wife, his nephew, and all of their possessions and started the long journey up the Euphrates River to the land that God would show him—the land of Canaan.

Significant moves are never easy. If you have ever made such a move, you know what I'm talking about. You left home, family, and familiarity to launch out on your own and find new directions, new places, new challenges—a new beginning. But most likely there was a time when uncertainty settled in. Apprehension overwhelmed you. You asked yourself, "Is this really what I want to do? I'm leaving everything behind."

Things weren't all that easy for Abram either. This new land was full of unfriendly strangers—Canaanites. There was also a famine, a disastrous trip to Egypt, and problems with the relatives. Then his nephew left, and eventually war broke out. I'm sure Abram began to wonder if he was ever going to have any children. Ten years went by, and still no kids.

That's when Abram came up with his own idea: adoption. It was perfectly acceptable in the ancient Near East to adopt a trusted servant as one's heir. Abram happened to have a great servant named Eliezer. So he approached God like this: "O Sovereign LORD, what can you give me since I remain childless and the one who will inherit my estate is Eliezer of Damascus?" Then Abram

> *God said it. I believe it! And that's how this journey of faith begins.*

continued, "You have given me no children; so a servant born in my household will be my heir" (Genesis 15:2,3).

Abram had presented his plan, but the Sovereign Lord had another idea. God replied, "This man will not be your heir, but a son coming from your own body will be your heir" (15:4). He would still have a son after all. Then God told Abram that his descendants would be as innumerable as the stars. "Count the stars," He challenged. "So shall your offspring be." What a promise!

That's when it happened! The Bible says, "Abram believed the LORD, and he credited it to him as righteousness" (15:6). That's when the promise became real to him. That's when he believed God in spite of his circumstances. God said it. That settles it. I believe it! And that's how the journey of faith begins for us too. Romans 4:5 puts it like this: "To the man . . . who trusts God . . . his faith is credited as righteousness."

How does faith begin? By believing. God has made us an offer—an offer to forgive our sins and to give us His righteousness as a free gift. Believing His offer to be sincere, we take that gift by faith. Believing that Jesus died for your sins, you claim it as your very own. You take Him as your Savior. In time, you will learn to walk and then to run. But you must begin by taking that first step. No more doubts. No more excuses. It's time to believe. Trust Him today.

Time Out

1. *Have I really taken that first step to know God?*

2. *Have I really committed my entire life to Jesus Christ?*

Making a Clear-Cut Decision

They had a unique way of settling things in the ancient world. Instead of "cutting a deal," they literally cut a covenant with each other. A covenant was an agreement. But "cutting" it was something else. They actually took animals and cut them in half. Then they laid the halves several feet across from each other, forming an aisle. Next, the two men making the covenant joined hands and walked together between the divided pieces.

What they were saying was, "I'll keep my half of the bargain, if you'll keep your half." The idea being that half of an animal wasn't worth anything. You can't get milk out of half a cow—especially if you have the wrong half! In other words, unless we cooperate, we'll never get the job done.

> *God had made an unconditional covenant with one man. The promise had been personalized. And the world would never be the same again!*

But notice what happened next. Genesis 15:12-18 tells us that God came down alone and "passed between the pieces." He did not take Abram's hand and walk together with him through the pieces. In fact, Abram was in a trance ("deep sleep") the whole time. This was not a conditional covenant. It was not an agreement that depended on both sides keeping their half of the bargain in order for it to work. God promised He would do it, and He did it—by Himself.

"On that day," the Bible says, "the LORD made a covenant with Abram" (Genesis 15:18). And God cut it deep. He promised Abram that his descendants would possess the entire land—the Promised Land. The land was the external evidence of God's commitment to keep His promise to Abram, which meant that it would belong to Abram's descendants forever.

It was a great day—a high and holy day. There had never been a day quite like it before. God had made an unconditional covenant with one man. The promise had been personalized. And the world would never be the same again!

Unconditional covenants are like marriage commitments. You make the vow for life and give your bride a ring to symbolize your commitment to her. You're not supposed to have the attitude that she can only keep the ring if she meets certain conditions. You are supposed to give it to her unconditionally. That's what God did with Abram. He made him an unconditional promise, and He is still keeping it today.

Don't Get Sidetracked

Abram undoubtedly came home excited. He had met with God, and God had promised him a son. But when he tried to explain it all to his wife, Sarai, something got lost in the translation. After all, he was 85 years old, and she was 75. She was too old to have children. Wasn't she?

"The LORD has kept me from having children," Sarai protested. "Go sleep with my maidservant; perhaps I can build a family through her," she suggested (Genesis 16:2).

That's when Plan B—a surrogate mother—went into action. "Maybe, you're going to have a baby, but I'm not!" is what Sarai was suggesting. Abram and Sarai put reason above revelation. God had clearly spoken, but it just didn't make sense to Sarai.

It was customary in the ancient world for a childless couple to have a child by a slave girl and adopt it as their own. However, this was merely a custom, not God's command. They chose to put human custom above the divine command. Abram gave in to Sarai's pressure and had a son by Hagar, their Egyptian maidservant. That son was Ishmael, the forefather of the Arabs.

"Hey, what could go wrong?" they reasoned. And 4000 years later, we are still asking, "Hey, what went wrong?" To this very day, the Arabs and the Jews hate each other, causing much controversy, terrorism, and unrest in the Middle East. Many of the problems that Israel faces today could have been avoided if Abram and Sarai had not taken God's plan into their own hands.

Every time we try to read between the lines of divine revelation, we do the same thing. We put reason above revelation, custom above the content of Scripture. And the end result is always trouble.

Look at Genesis 16:16. It's the last verse of the chapter. It says, "Abram was eighty-six years old when Hagar bore him Ishmael." Now look at the next verse—Genesis 17:1. It says that God appeared to him when he was "ninety-nine years old." Subtract the difference. It's 13 years.

For 13 years there is no new message from God. What happened during those silent years? We don't know. But you can't read these verses without getting the distinct impression that God stopped talking to Abram. He wasn't listening, so God stopped talking.

Divine revelation came to a screeching halt. Abram muddled on the best he could, wondering what had happened to the promise. In the meantime, God waited for a better time.

Halftime

1. *Think of the times when you tried to run ahead of God's timing in your life. What went wrong?*

2. *How long were you sidetracked? And what did God have to do to get your attention?*

A New Beginning

After 13 years of silence, God spoke to Abram. He was now 99 years old. Ishmael was a teenager. The promised son had not yet been born, but God's intention had not changed. He still planned for Abram and Sarai to have a son of their own.

"I am God Almighty [Hebrew, *El Shaddai*]," the Lord announced to Abram. "I will confirm my covenant between me and you and will greatly increase your numbers" (Genesis 17:1,2).

Abram fell on his face before God. The long wait was over. All he could do was listen.

"No longer will you be called Abram; your name will be Abraham ["father of multitudes"], for I have made you a father of many nations," explained God (17:5).

God went on to tell Abraham that He was making an "everlasting covenant" with him and his descendants to give them the land of Canaan. Then He explained that circumcision would be the sign of that covenant. It would be a mark in their flesh to remind the generations to come that every descendant of theirs was to be dedicated to God.

Then God changed Sarai's name to Sarah ("princess"). "I will bless her," God promised, "and will surely give you a son by her" (17:16). God graciously reconfirmed everything He had told Abraham 13 years earlier, and clearly reemphasized that he would have a son by Sarah.

Abraham should have been thrilled. But the Bible says, "He laughed and said to himself, 'Will a son be born to a man a hundred years old? Will Sarah bear a child at the age of ninety?'" (17:17). Then Abraham appealed to God to let Ishmael be the promised son.

God replied that He would bless Ishmael, but that the covenant would be made with their new son—Isaac (which means "laughter"). "You think this is funny? Let's see who's laughing now. Name the boy 'laughter.' When? By this time next year, you *will* have a son." Then God "went up" and disappeared.

I believe this was the ultimate turning point for Abraham. He had been given a second chance, and he knew it. Back to Plan A—no more messing around, no more laughing at God. It was time to get serious, and he knew it.

Telling Your Wife the Truth

There is no doubt Abraham went home a new man, with a new name, with a renewed faith and a new confidence. However, he made one major error. He didn't bother to tell Sarah about it.

"She'll never believe it!" he probably thought.

Like a lot of men, Abraham made his peace with God, but he remained a spiritual "secret agent" at home. "No use getting the little woman all upset," thought Abraham. "She's got enough pressures on her. Besides, she'll just think I made the whole thing up. I'll just keep quiet and see what happens."

But God wouldn't let him keep quiet. He decided if Abraham wasn't going to tell Sarah, He would. In Genesis 18, we read the story of God and two angels visiting Abraham's tent at Mamre (modern Hebron).

Abraham looked up one day and saw three strangers coming his way. Strangers! Visitors! Time for some good old Near East hospitality. He bows and greets them and welcomes them into the shade of the great tree before his tent. Then there was a flurry of activity. Sarah ran to make bread, and Abraham ran to catch dinner.

Later, when the men settled down to eat dinner, they asked, "Where is your wife, Sarah?"

"There, in the tent," Abraham replied.

The stranger lifted his head to speak: "I will surely return to you about this time next year, and Sarah your wife will have a son."

It was the Lord Himself! Abraham sat speechless.

Now Sarah could hear them talking outside the tent, and she laughed to herself because she was "past the age of childbearing" (18:11). It wasn't even physically possible for her to get pregnant. It would take a miracle for her to have a baby!

"Why did Sarah laugh?" the Lord asked. But Abraham just sat there in shocked silence.

"I did not laugh," Sarah protested, apparently sticking her head out of the tent.

"Yes, you did," the Lord said. "Is anything too hard for the Lord?"

That was it. They finished the meal and got up to leave. The two angels had serious business to attend to in Sodom, so they went on their way. Abraham talked with God a little longer, and then He was gone.

The Promise Fulfilled

Time passed, and sure enough, Sarah got pregnant. It was humanly impossible, but it happened. It was a miracle of God's grace. Nine months later, the miracle-born son arrived. And they called his name Isaac.

They had laughed at God, but now they were laughing with Him. The promise was real. It had been kept. Their son had been born. Their faith had been confirmed. Isaac was the son of the promise—the son of the covenant, the forefather of the Jews, the ancestor of the people of God.

Isaac, the miracle-born son of Abraham, was also destined to become the forefather of another miracle-born son of Abraham, Jesus Christ, the virgin-born Messiah. He, too, would enter the human race by unconventional means—this time without a human father. Isaac would begin a miraculous line of people, and Jesus would be the culmination of all their hopes and dreams.

It was a great day when Isaac was born. No one could have been happier than Abraham. He had believed God and trusted Him. Though his faith had been challenged by his circumstances, he was now completely committed to God. He knew the Promisor, and that made all the difference.

The Final Challenge

For the next 20 years, Isaac was the joy of their lives. They watched him grow into a young man. But then one day God decided to put the promise to the ultimate test.

"Take your son, your only son Isaac, whom you love, and go to the region of Moriah," God commanded Abraham. "Sacrifice him there as a burnt offering on one of the mountains" (Genesis 22:2).

Human sacrifice! It was totally contrary to the nature and character of God. A "burnt offering" meant killing the sacrifice and burning it up completely as an offering to God. The Hebrew term for it was *hola*, from which we get the word *holocaust*. Nothing could have been more inappropriate for the father of the Jews!

In every journey of faith, there comes that crucial moment when everything you believe is put to the test.

You don't find Abraham laughing this time. No excuses. No explanations. No hesitation. He saddled his donkey, chopped the wood, took two servants along with Isaac, and set out for Moriah. He was now 120 years old. He had walked with God a long time. He had come to realize that the Promisor was greater than the promise. And this was no time to doubt the Promisor.

I believe with all my heart that Abraham knew that God would keep the promise. The boy can't die. He's the fulfillment. There can't be a Jewish race without Him—no Promised Land, no future Messiah, no Savior, no salvation! That is why Abraham told the servants to wait with the donkey. Then he added: "I and the boy ... will worship and then we will come back to you" (Genesis 22:5).

In every journey of faith, there comes that crucial moment when everything you believe is put to the test. We want the blessings all right. But do we really want the One who blesses more than the blessing? Only when we face that question for ourselves are we really ready to move on by faith. Our journey with God begins by faith. It must also continue by faith.

When God Provides

When Isaac questions where the lamb is for the sacrifice, Abraham simply replies, "God himself will provide the lamb" (Genesis 22:8). Here is faith at its best. Abraham knows God must provide a substitute or else raise this boy back from the dead. One or the other—He can't let him die. He promised! That's why they later call the place of sacrifice *Jehovah Jireh,* "the Lord provides."

They arrived at the rocky summit of the hill—ironically, at the very place where the altar of sacrifice would later stand in the Temple. Here at this point, an incredible act took place. Isaac *willingly* allowed his aged father to bind him and lay him on the altar. He could have easily resisted, but he did not. He was obedient even unto death.

Willing, if necessary, to do whatever God asked, yet desperately believing the Promisor would provide, Abraham took the knife and raised it above his son. Only then did the angel of the Lord (Christ Himself) call from heaven.

"Do not lay a hand on the boy," He said. "Now I know that you fear God, because you have not withheld from me your son, your only son" (22:12).

When Abraham turned, he saw a ram caught by its horns in a thicket. God had indeed provided the substitute for the burnt offering. Isaac was set free.

There would come a day, 20 centuries later, when God would bring His only Son to that same place. He too would carry the wood—the cross. He too would willingly be bound—with our sins. He too would be placed on the altar of sacrifice, and the hand of the Father would be raised against Him.

But this time, there would be no one to call from heaven. And God's hand of judgment would fall on Jesus—the ultimate substitute, the eternal sacrifice, the only Son of the divine Father. God would do to His Son what He would not let Abraham do to his son. Jesus would be put to death as the ultimate sacrifice—the Lamb of God, slain from the foundation of the world.

That's when the promise began. In the mind and heart of God, in the aeons of eternity past. As He foresaw our great need, His divine grace moved to meet that need. So He created the perfect plan, and sent His Son to redeem the world.

God gave everything He had for us. The least we can do is give ourselves to Him. That's all He really wants—you! And He will take you just as you are; with all your sins, failures, and defeats; with your broken life and broken promises. He will take you however you come and make you a brand-new man—a man of the promise.

Postgame Highlights

1. *Am I willing to put everything on the altar of sacrifice?*

2. *What do I seem to want to hold back?*

3. *Is holding back really worth it?*

Personal Interview

If I really let God have total control of my life, what would I have to be willing to do?

_____

_____

_____

_____

Final Wrap-up

Faith doesn't change my circumstances.
It changes me.

–John Maxwell

Overcoming the Obstacles:

Hanging Tough in the Tough Times

Everything rises and falls on leadership!" How many times have we heard that statement? It is so true that it has become a maxim by which whole corporations are run. Whatever is wrong with the organization is almost always a reflection of what is wrong with the leader. It's true on the corporate level. And it's true on the personal level as well.

The success or failure of leadership shows up first of all in the home. When the father is not the spiritual leader he ought to be, the whole family suffers. If he doesn't set the example, there will always be conflicts that could have been avoided.

God calls men to be leaders at home, in the church, and in the community. But we will never succeed at church or in the community until we succeed at home. Being the right kind of husband and father is essential to having the right kind of family. It won't work fully without godly male leadership.

Men need to become leaders at home as well as at work. The biblical plan is for the father to be the head of the home. His loving leadership is intended to build a canopy of protection over his wife and children. But with the privilege of leadership comes the responsibility of leadership.

The husband's responsibilities toward his wife include:

1. Love her (Ephesians 5:25).
2. Honor her (1 Peter 3:7).
3. Trust her (Proverbs 31:11).
4. Praise her (Proverbs 31:28).
5. Sanctify her (1 Corinthians 7:14).
6. Protect her (Ruth 1:9).
7. Provide for her (1 Timothy 5:8).
8. Teach her (1 Corinthians 14:34,35).
9. Cheer her (Ecclesiastes 9:9).
10. Befriend her (Song of Solomon 5:16).

As fathers, men also have basic duties to fulfill in a biblically based Christian family. We need to set the example for our children by modeling the attitudes and behaviors we expect from them. Raising children has never been easy, but it has always been rewarding. Parenting is one of the greatest joys of life, both for us and for our children.

Dad's responsibilities toward his children include providing:

1. Positive example (Psalm 103:8-13).
2. Spiritual heritage (1 Peter 1:4).
3. Financial security (2 Corinthians 12:14).
4. Biblical instruction (Deuteronomy 6:6-9).
5. Consistent discipline (Proverbs 22:6).
6. Practical advice (Ephesians 6:4).
7. Future blessing (Mark 10:13-16).

A Divided Family

After Abraham died, Isaac received confirmation from God that the promise given to his father, Abraham, would continue through his family line. The Bible tells us that Isaac had twin sons—Esau and Jacob. However, they were not identical twins. Esau, the eldest, was the rugged, masculine, macho type. He had red hair—lots of it—all over his body, which fit his masculine image. He quickly became his father's favorite because he loved the outdoors—especially hunting

When the father is not the spiritual leader he ought to be, the whole family suffers.

and everything that goes with it. Isaac was the typical proud father who enjoyed reliving his youth through his son.

Jacob, on the other hand, was a quiet, smooth-skinned boy, less rugged. And definitely not an outdoorsman. The Bible says that he was Mama's favorite. He liked to hang around the kitchen and help prepare the food. But the favoritism of Dad toward Esau and Mom toward Jacob created division in the family. Eventually that division surfaced as rivalry and competitiveness between the boys.

Isaac and Rebekah lived very prosperous and peaceful lives—except for their two sons. Esau and Jacob were at each other constantly. They wore their parents out. And they brought pain and heartache to their lives.

In ancient Near Eastern families, two traditions were vitally important. When the father was about to die, he always gave his eldest son the birthright and the blessing. The *birthright* automatically gave the eldest the position of leadership in the family when the father passed on. The *blessing* meant he received a double portion of his father's inheritance. In other words, he got twice as much as the other brothers.

Ripped Off by Your Own Brother

One day Esau came home from a long, unsuccessful day of hunting. He was absolutely famished! He didn't catch anything to eat. Meanwhile, Jacob has been at home all day making a big pot of chili, or red bean soup as the Bible describes it. Jacob teased with Esau: "Hey, Big Red, did ya catch anything today?"

"I didn't catch anything, Mama's Boy, and I'm starving. Give me some of that red stuff." Esau reached for the chili, but Jacob pulled it away.

"First sell me your birthright," insisted Jacob (Genesis 25:31). Now Jacob might have been joking. However, there is usually a little truth behind every good joke. In Hebrew, Jacob's name means "a conniver, a manipulator, a deceiver." In literal terms it is translated "a supplanter"—one who steals the place of someone else. And remember, in this family there's a big inheritance at stake.

Esau was so hungry he didn't care. Genesis 25:34 says that he "despised his birthright." He took it lightly. "What good is the birthright to me when I'm about to die of hunger?" So he exchanged his birthright for the bowl of soup. He probably figured he could beat Jacob up anytime he needed to anyway. But God noted a character flaw in Esau's attitude. Esau did not take the responsibility of leadership seriously.

There has always been an argument over whether leaders are *born* leaders or whether they *become* leaders. Certainly some men seem to show leadership qualities from a very early age. Natural gifts, talents, and physical prowess can lend themselves to one's success. Esau was certainly born with a natural physical advantage.

But leaders are also made and developed by their response to their natural circumstances. Some, like Jacob, have to learn to lead. In fact, his physical weakness caused him to develop a psychological edge over his brother.

The Ultimate Deception

Time passed and Isaac became ill. His eyesight was failing him. In fact, he was nearly blind. Besides, he thought he was going to die. According to ancient tradition, they didn't write down their last will and testament. They gave it verbally. So Isaac called Esau in to give him his blessing. "Son," Isaac said, "I want you to go hunt some wild game for me. Prepare it how I like it so I can have one last good meal, and I will give you the blessing before I die."

Now the Bible says that Rebekah was eavesdropping the whole time. She ran to Jacob, her favorite, and said, "We've got to do something! Your brother is going to get the blessing! Why don't you go in and tell him you're Esau? I'll fix some venison the way he likes it. You can take your meal in first, and beat your brother to the blessing."

"But Esau is big and tough and hairy. What if father reaches out to touch me and figures out who I am?" questioned Jacob.

"We'll put goat skins on your arms so if he touches you, he'll think you're Esau for sure. Remember, he's practically blind!" replied Rebekah.

Sure enough, they deceived old dad. Isaac unknowingly gave the blessing to the wrong son–Jacob. However, the irony of all of this is that before the twins were born, God had predicted that "the older [Esau] would serve the younger [Jacob]" (25:23). It was God's original plan for Jacob to have the blessing. God knew that Esau would not be a responsible leader before he was even born. But instead of waiting for God to work it all out, Rebekah and Jacob interfered and took matters into their own hands. They tried to do it their way, but they ended up creating a mess. Remember, there are no real shortcuts to success.

When Esau returned and discovered that Jacob had stolen the blessing, he was furious! "Isn't he rightly named Jacob [deceiver]? He has deceived me these two times: He took my birthright, and now he's taken my blessing!" Esau vowed to kill Jacob, so Isaac and Rebekah were forced to send Jacob away. Now the family was divided not only by favoritism and rivalry, but by physical distance as well. And, tragically, Rebekah never saw Jacob again.

Time Out

1. *What things are threatening division in your family?*

2. *Are you part of the solution or part of the problem?*

Deceiver Meets Keeper of Promises

Jacob left home in a hurry, promising to return in "a few days." But he was gone for 20 years.

Jacob fled from Esau to Haran, in Syria, where his Uncle Laban (Rebekah's brother) lived. En route between Beersheba and Haran, Jacob stopped to rest for the night. The Scripture says that he used a stone for a pillow (no wonder he had a dream!). He dreamt that a stairway (KJV, "ladder") came down from heaven with angels ascending and descending on it. At the top of the stairway, the Lord stood and said, "I am the LORD, the God of your father Abraham and the God of Isaac" (Genesis 28:13).

Notice, God did not say "I am your God" to Jacob. Because He wasn't. Jacob's life was a mess! He had tricked his brother out of the birthright, stolen the blessing by deceiving his father, and now he was running for his life. He was leaving the very land he had hoped to inherit by stealing the blessing. But God intervened. He came to renew the promise He had made to Abraham and Isaac. God implies that He is willing to be Jacob's God also.

God said, "I will give you and your descendants the land on which you are lying.... I am with you and will watch over you wherever you go, and I will bring you back to this land. I will not leave you until I have done what I have promised you" (28:13-15).

What amazing grace! What an amazing promise! God was telling Jacob that He would stay with him and take care of him and bring him back to where He planned for him to be. God was promising to do for Jacob what he could not do for himself—bless him, protect him, and bring him home again.

God does not expect us to be perfect to receive His promises. He meets us right where we are because we could never get to where He is. Just like God promised to help Jacob, He promises to help us. There is nothing we can do to cause God *not* to keep His promises. He is the ultimate Keeper of Promises! Second Timothy 2:13 tells us that even "if we are faithless, he will remain faithful, for he cannot disown himself." He cannot be anything else but faithful to His promises.

Jacob woke up, but instead of being excited about God's presence, he was scared to death! He was afraid because he had seen God face-to-face. Usually when we have sin in our lives, we are not in a big hurry to see God face-to-face because we know that our guilt will be exposed. But we need to have our sin exposed in order to recognize our need for God to remove it and replace it with His grace.

A New Direction

Considering the number of mistakes he had already made, Jacob finally made a wise choice. He came to a point of genuine conversion. He totally committed his life to God, saying, "The LORD will be my God...and of all that you give me I will give you a tenth" (Genesis 28:21,22). The fact that he promised to tithe is dramatic evidence that he had been changed. The *taker* promised to become a *giver*. And that meant a whole new direction in his life.

Then Jacob did something else unusual to indicate his commitment to God. He built an altar of worship. On that altar he poured out oil, which he had carried for his long journey. It was the only valuable thing he had with him. He did not have an animal sacrifice. He simply gave all that he had. And poured it out on the altar. He called that place Bethel, which in the Hebrew language means "the house of God." There was no building there. There was no structure there. It was just a hillside on the edge of the Canaanite city of Luz. But it was the place where Jacob met God, so he called it "the house of God."

Our relationship to the house of God tends to run parallel to our relationship with God.

I have observed over the years that our relationship to the house of God tends to run parallel to our relationship with God. When we are in a right relationship with God, we enjoy being in God's house. But when we are not in a right relationship with God, we do not want to be in the house of God. So when people say, "I've kind of gotten out of the church," what they really mean is, "I've gotten away from God."

Where were you when you came to know the Lord? I have asked this question to audiences all over the United States. The vast majority raise their hands to indicate that they were saved in a church or in a church-related service. Far more were converted in the house of God than in a camp or citywide rally or something else. I have come to the conclusion that while God blesses parachurch evangelistic enterprises, most people meet the Lord in a local church. In the house of God where the Word of God is faithfully proclaimed week after week.

When you experience true conversion, the place where you meet God, the house of God, becomes the most important place in your life. Likewise, Bethel became the most important place in Jacob's life. It would mark every major turning point in his walk with God.

Halftime

1. *Is your relationship with God what it should be right now?*

2. *Is your relationship with the house of God (your local church) what it should be right now?*

What Goes Around Comes Around

I will never forget the feeling of becoming a father for the very first time. My wife and I invested every spare minute we had into our innocent little angel. Although she changed our lives dramatically, she was still our beautiful, perfect little girl–Linda.

A few years later, I came home from work one day, kissed my wife as usual, but this time she burst into tears. "What's wrong?" I asked calmly.

In between sobs she said, "It's Linda...she...she..."

I immediately panicked. "Is she all right? What happened? Did she fall? Did she get hurt? Where is she?"

Still crying uncontrollably, Donna managed to reply, "She...*stole* something, and then she...*lied* to me!"

Linda, our three-year-old "angel," had refused to eat her lunch. As a result, my wife refused to give her a chocolate Popsicle for dessert. While Mom was out of the room, little

Linda sneaked into the kitchen. She stole a chocolate Popsicle out of the freezer. Then she gobbled it down and threw the empty stick and wrapper in the trash can. But she forgot one minor detail: the chocolate mustache across her lips. It was a sure giveaway!

What really hurt Donna was that, in spite of the evidence, Linda lied about what she had done. Even after my wife retrieved the empty wrapper from the trash can, Linda insisted she didn't know where it came from. It was our first parental lesson in human depravity.

About a year ago, I was talking to our daughter Linda on the phone. She's now a married woman with a daughter of her own. "Dad, you'll never believe what happened," she said in a shaky voice. "I don't know what I've done wrong! Jennifer (her three-year-old daughter) cut the neighbor girl's bangs off!"

I couldn't help but laugh! I reminded Linda that she had done the same kind of thing at the same age. It wasn't much comfort to her. But it reminded me that "what goes around, comes around."

Jacob had come to a turning point in his life at Bethel. But he still had some tough obstacles to face. And a lot of growing to do. The consequences of the bad choices he had made earlier in life were about to catch up to him. When he got to Haran, he received a "taste of his own medicine."

Jacob arrived in Haran looking for his Uncle Laban. He didn't have a telephone directory, and there were no street addresses. So he went to the well on the edge of town, hoping to find somebody who could direct him to Laban's house. When he arrived at the well, the young single girls of the city were coming out to water the sheep. Somebody had left the stone on the mouth of the well, and the girls couldn't roll the stone away.

"Jacob thought, "Aha, here's a chance to show off my muscles and impress the girls."

"Step aside, ladies. I'll roll the stone away. No sweat!"

He rolled the stone away, and caught eyes with one girl who really made his adrenaline flow. It was love at first sight! In fact, he ran right up and kissed her! Genesis 29:11 says, "Jacob kissed Rachel and began to weep aloud." I don't know if he was disappointed, or if she bit him on the lip! Acually they were both overjoyed to meet one another. Jacob probably wept because he was relieved to find someone who cared about him.

Love at First Sight

Jacob soon discovered that Rachel was Laban's daughter. She was his cousin. Actually, his "kissing cousin" now. "I've traveled a long way to find your daddy," Jacob might have said. "Did I mention that my parents wanted me to find a wife among your people while I'm here?"

"This is great! You can stay with us. We have plenty of room!" replied Rachel, looking like she had just won the lottery.

Rachel took Jacob home to Laban. Now Laban was thrilled to see Jacob because he remembered years ago when Abraham sent an entourage up to Haran to find a wife for Isaac. They had selected his sister, Rebekah. But most of all, he remembered all of the gold and silver and precious goods that they had brought. Laban literally ran to meet Jacob.

"Jacob! So good to see you! How's your money—I mean your family?" Little did he know that Jacob had left home in a hurry and didn't bring anything with him—not even a credit card!

Jacob fell in love with Rachel. One day he mustered up the courage to ask Laban if he could marry her. He didn't have any money for a dowry, so he agreed to work for Laban for seven years to pay for the dowry. Jacob was so madly in love that the Bible says he "served seven years to get Rachel, but they seemed like only a few days to him because of his love for her" (Genesis 29:20). He lost all sense of time. But it made him forget about all his problems back home. Finally, the day of the wedding arrived.

In the Near East, the bride was traditionally covered in veils during the marriage celebration. Realistically, you couldn't even tell what she looked like. Some fathers may have started this tradition so they could get rid of their daughters! Well, Laban decided that he couldn't allow the younger daughter to marry before her older sister, Leah. So Laban switched brides. Because of all of the veils, poor Jacob didn't even realize that he had the wrong girl until the next morning.

Getting What We Deserve

The great "deceiver" was deceived! He found out what it felt like to be taken for a fool. He complained to Laban, "What have you done? You gave me Leah, and I wanted Rachel!" But it was too late. It was then that Jacob made his next big mistake. Instead of seeking God's will or waiting to see if maybe God had picked Leah, he made a decision and created another mess. If you read all of Genesis 29, you will discover that Jacob made his decision without ever praying or asking God what to do.

Jacob decided to marry both girls. He agreed to work another seven years for Rachel. But he married her as soon as the required seven-day honeymoon with Leah was over (verse 28). Now Jacob was married to two jealous sisters. Trying to earn his favor, they entered into the greatest childbearing contest known in the history of mankind. Within eight years, he fathered 12 sons and a daughter.

From its beginning, Jacob's family was split by division. Favoritism and rivalry ruled the house. And it was far worse than anything he and Esau had ever experienced back home.

Men, by nature, like to fix things. When my wife tells me about a problem, she usually just wants me to listen. But I don't want to listen. I want to fix it. We like to feel as if we are capable of fixing any problem that happens in our family. However, our biggest problem is that sometimes we cannot see God's plan, and it's impossible to fix what you can't see.

Jacob couldn't see God's plan for Leah in his life. He only saw the problem—I've got the wrong wife! He did not realize that Leah would become the mother of Judah. And from the line of Judah would come David, and from the line of David would come Jesus—the ultimate fulfillment of God's promise. That's right! Jesus Christ came from Leah and not from Rachel!

Because Jacob had interfered again, everything went wrong. Not only was Jacob's own family divided, but Laban got angry with Jacob as well. The 14 years of labor finally passed. Laban started paying Jacob for his work, but he unfairly changed Jacob's wages and cheated him every time he had a chance. Then he complained that Jacob was stealing his cattle and cheating him. Once again, Jacob's life was a mess!

Turning Back to God

In spite of his mess, God blessed Jacob as He had promised and caused his flocks and his wealth to multiply. Then God appeared to Jacob to remind him that He was still with him and said, "I am the God of Bethel, where you anointed a pillar and where you made a vow to me. Now leave this land at once and go back to your native land" (Genesis 31:13). God did not literally say, "Go back to Bethel," but His command implies that it was time for Jacob to go back to the "house of God."

Instead of trusting God and facing Laban, Jacob "escaped" while his uncle was out of town. Laban pursued him, but God convinced Laban to let Jacob and all of his family go. Surprise! God changed Laban's heart! He could have changed it in the first place, but Jacob didn't want to wait for Him to do it. Instead, he ran away–just like he had run from Esau.

While Jacob was on his way back to Canaan, another problem occurred to him–Esau! What if Esau still wanted to kill him? Again, Jacob didn't ask God about it. Instead, he sent messengers ahead of him to talk to Esau to find out if he was still angry. The messengers returned and reported, "Esau your brother is coming to meet you, and he's bringing 400 men with him." Four hundred men! Jacob panicked! Then he did something really brave and heroic. He sent his wives and his children on ahead, while he stayed in the back.

It was that very night that the angel of the Lord appeared to Jacob and physically wrestled with him. They wrestled all night long. Jacob kept saying, "I will not let you go unless you bless me." He was already guilty of stealing the blessing from his brother, and now he was struggling to keep the blessing of God in his life. He was going about it all wrong! He was going after the blessing by his own power. God's blessing isn't something we can earn by our own merit. It is something He gives us by His grace.

The angel finally blessed Jacob and said, "Your name will no longer be Jacob, but Israel" (Genesis 32:28). Israel means "a prince with God." It also became the name of God's chosen nation. Jacob would struggle with waiting on God for the rest of his life, but God would still keep His promise to make him into a mighty nation. Jacob left this encounter limping. His physical condition was altered as a reminder that he had struggled with God. And it was also a reminder that God would still fulfill His promise in spite of Jacob's failures.

Later, Jacob caught up to his family and finally met Esau. It had been 20 years. Esau ran up to him and hugged him and wept. Obviously, God had changed his heart.

Esau expressed his greetings and asked, "Whose kids are all these kids?"

"They're mine!" Jacob replied.

"You can't fit all these kids into Dad's house," Esau may have said. "Why don't you move in with me, down in Edom?"

Jacob thought, "I'm not going anywhere near that place! I'll get down there alone with him, and he'll try to kill me!" Again, he didn't talk to God about it. He told Esau, "You go ahead and tell your family that we're coming. We'll be there in a few days."

Afterward, Jacob turned and headed the opposite way. At this point, Jacob was only about ten miles from Bethel, but instead of going on to Bethel, he turned around and went 20 miles north. Again, he took his problem into his own hands. Besides, what could go wrong?

Jacob settled his family just outside of the ungodly Canaanite city of Shechem, and everything went wrong. His daughter Dinah was kidnapped and raped. Then his sons killed every man in the town to get revenge. And once again Jacob is in trouble! Again he had to run for his life.

Going All the Way

Finally, in desperation, Jacob cried out to God. And God appeared to him one more time. "Go up to Bethel and settle there, and build an altar to God," the Lord instructed him. God also told Jacob to get his family in order. "Put away the strange gods," He told them, "and change your clothes."

This time Jacob listened. He gathered his family together and demanded that they give up their idols, change their clothes, and start looking and acting like God's people. He finally became the leader that God wanted him to be. And he marched his family back to Bethel.

It was time to come back to the "house of God." Jacob had been away for too long. Even though he got close to it, he didn't get close enough. This time, he really meant business with God and went all the way.

When Jacob arrived at Bethel, he built an altar to God. But this time he did not call it Bethel. This time he called it

El Bethel which means the God of the house of God (Genesis 35:7). Jacob was making it clear to his family that he was not just "going back to church." He was going back to God. He was going back to the God of the "house of God."

From this point on, God began to turn Jacob's life around. He had sown some pretty bad seeds that still surfaced from time to time, but God was finally able to begin turning him around.

Going back to church will not change your life. But going back to God will.

Jacob had to learn that going back to church will not change your life. But going back to God will. It was the Person, not the place, that changed his life. Going to church, joining the church, volunteering to be an usher or to sing in the choir are all good things. But they won't change your life. Coming back to church may be the first step in the right direction. But it's only the first step. You may need to come back to God Himself.

At the end of Jacob's life he said, "My years have been few and difficult" (Genesis 47:9). God had a plan for Jacob before he was even born. Unfortunately, Jacob often interfered with God's plan and brought unnecessary suffering into his life. Instead of waiting on God to give him the blessing, he took it by deception. In return, he himself was deceived by Laban and later by his own sons.

Jacob spent years running for his life, instead of trusting God's promises. But God graciously pursued him until He brought him home. And that same God will pursue you until you surrender to His will and plan for your life.

Postgame Highlights

1. *Take a minute to reflect on the time and the place where you first met God.*

2. *What obstacles or difficulties have come into your life since then?*

3. *Are any of those difficulties still unresolved?*

Personal Interview

If you could change the way your life has turned out, what would you do differently?

_____

_____

_____

_____

Final Wrap-up

You do not determine a man's greatness by his talent or his wealth as the world does, but rather by what it takes to discourage him.

–Jerry Falwell

When Dreams and Heroes Die:

Starting Over When It All Falls Apart

Bob and Sandy appeared to have the typical all-American family. Two kids. Great jobs. Upward mobility. A measure of success. And some financial security. It all looked great—on the surface. Then the bomb dropped. She ran off with his best friend.

"I was so shocked I couldn't begin to deal with it," Bob told me. "I just walked around in complete confusion. I felt totally abandoned!"

Sandy divorced Bob. Eventually, she married Bob's friend, who was in the military. What was worse, they took Bob's two children and got transferred to Iceland. For the next five years, Bob never saw any of them.

By the time Bob had any interaction with the kids, they were already grown. Time and distance had placed a barrier between them. When he did see them, he felt estranged from them. But he couldn't figure out why. He assumed they just didn't want a relationship with him any longer.

It was years later, after the girls married, that Bob finally began to realize what had happened. Not only did he feel abandoned by their mother, but they felt abandoned by him. They never saw him. So they lost contact.

Only as adults did the girls begin to realize that their mother kept them isolated from their father. She didn't want to have to deal with Bob. So she (and the girls) stayed away—deliberately. In the girl's minds, dad just seemed to disappear from their lives.

> *Being abandoned, for whatever reason, hurts so deeply that it is difficult to deal with.*

The real tragedy with divorce is that it hurts so many people. Bob felt abandoned by his wife. The kids felt abandoned by their dad. And Bob felt abandoned by his own children.

Being abandoned, for whatever reason, hurts so deeply that it is difficult to deal with. Anyone who has ever been hurt by rejection, betrayal, or divorce knows the pain of feeling abandoned. Feeling helpless, hopeless, and all alone.

Most of us don't deal with that kind of pain very well. It is easy for hurting people to hurt people. We want revenge. We want to lash out at someone else. Often we become a powder keg of emotions waiting to explode.

Daddy's Boy

That's what makes the story of Joseph so unique. He was the son of Jacob and Rachel. Her firstborn. And Jacob's favorite. You would think that after all Jacob went through with his father favoring his brother, Jacob would have been more careful. But he wasn't. Leah's sons were such a disappointment to him that he quickly favored Joseph over the others.

Joseph had the advantage of growing up after his father's spiritual turning point at Bethel. Unlike his half brothers who had witnessed Jacob's conniving and manipulative lifestyle, Joseph was raised by a dad whose life had been dramatically transformed by God. So Joseph grew up respecting his father and following his godly example.

Joseph's brothers were another story altogether. They were liars, deceivers, manipulators—and those were some of their better qualities! They had even committed murder. By contrast, Joseph was a "goody-goody" and a "daddy's boy." So it was inevitable that there would be problems between them.

The family eventually left Bethel and migrated south toward Bethlehem (Genesis 35:16-20). En route, Rachel, who was pregnant, delivered her second son, Benjamin. But in the process of the delivery, she died. Jacob was heartbroken over the loss of his favorite wife. And Joseph experienced the first pains of feeling abandoned.

To make up for his mother's loss, Jacob showered Joseph with presents, like his multicolored coat. The problem was that such treatment only caused his half brothers to resent him all the more. And then there were his constant dreams about all of them bowing down to him, which only made matters worse.

The Dream Becomes a Nightmare

When Joseph was 17 years old, a crisis occurred that changed his life forever. His ten brothers took the family flocks north to graze them near Shechem. After a while, Jacob asked Joseph to go and check on them and the sheep.

When Joseph arrived in the region, he was told his brothers had moved on to Dothan. So he went looking for them. But when they saw him coming, they resented his intrusion so much that they plotted to kill him.

"Here comes that dreamer!" they shouted. "Come now, let's kill him and throw him into one of these cisterns and say that a ferocious animal devoured him. Then we'll see what comes of his dreams" (Genesis 37:19,20).

Reuben, the eldest, tried to rescue him, but to no avail. Then Judah suggested they sell him to a passing caravan of Arab traders. Good idea! They all agreed. And Joseph was sold into slavery for 20 pieces of silver.

To cover their ill-gotten gain, the brothers tore up the colorful robe and soaked it in goat's blood. When Jacob saw the bloody robe, he assumed Joseph had been eaten by a wild animal. Again, the deceiver was deceived. This time by his own sons.

Jacob's grief was so great that he refused to be comforted. He sobbed uncontrollably. "In mourning will I go down to the grave to my son," he insisted.

The real tragedy was that Jacob remained in agony over this deception for 20 years. The same amount of time he had been separated from his parents when he fled from Esau. In the meantime, Joseph had plenty of problems of his own.

Time Out

1. Have you ever felt betrayed or abandoned?

2. How did you handle it? How are you handling it now?

From the Pit to the Prison

The Arabs eventually sold Joseph into slavery in Egypt. In the providence of God, he was purchased by an Egyptian official, Potiphar, the captain of Pharaoh's guard. And he was taken to Potiphar's house, where he quickly rose to the position of chief steward and his master's personal attendant.

But it wasn't long until new problems arose. Potiphar's wife took an interest in Joseph. Perhaps she was bored and felt neglected by her busy husband. Or perhaps she was attracted to Joseph's handsome physique. Whatever the reason, she risked telling him how she felt.

"Come to bed with me," she suggested.

But Joseph refused. He had already witnessed enough heartaches in his own family from illicit affairs.

"How then could I do such a wicked thing and sin against God?" he protested (Genesis 39:9).

The biblical account indicates that she kept at him day after day. Most men would have given in to the temptation: *He's gone. There's no one home. We're both adults. Besides, she needs it. Why not? What harm could it do?*

Not Joseph. He stood his ground. Refusing her advances day after day. That's where we see what this young man is made of. The depth of his character was impeccable. And his confidence in God was incredible. Most other men would have been bitter. They would have blamed God. And they would have given in to temptation.

> *The real test of human character comes when the bottom falls out of our lives.*

The real test of human character comes when the bottom falls out of our lives. That's when our faith in God is challenged: *Can I still trust after everything that has happened to me? If He really loves me, how can He even let this happen to me? Living for Him just isn't paying off!*

When Joseph continued to refuse his master's wife, she turned on him with a vengeance. First, she threw herself at him. But he ran off, leaving his cloak in her hands. He got into more trouble over his clothes! Angered by his rejection she went to her husband and falsely accused Joseph of attempting to seduce her.

Being a slave meant you were very susceptible to an accusation. He had no legal recourse. He was condemned and thrown into the royal dungeon. But even there, Joseph refused to turn against God. He became a model prisoner. In time, he was made the warden's assistant.

From Prison to the Palace

We don't know the exact time line of all the details in Joseph's life. But we do know he was sold by his brothers when he was 17 (Genesis 37:2). And he languished in prison until he was 30 (41:46). Thirteen years passed until his big break came.

Think of all that Joseph had been through:
1. Painful death of his mother.
2. Jealous resentment of his brothers.
3. Betrayal and abandonment by his family.
4. Humiliation of human slavery.
5. False accusation and imprisonment.

Despite all this, he never gave up on God. There was no hint of bitterness or hostility. In every situation, Joseph rose above his circumstances by the power of God.

Genesis 40 records the story of Pharaoh's butler and baker being thrown into the royal dungeon and their personal encounter with Joseph. He interpreted their dreams and begged them to plead his innocence to Pharaoh. Even though the interpretations came true, the butler (cupbearer) forgot about Joseph for two more years. Finally, a crisis occurred when Pharaoh had a troubling dream of his own (Genesis 41:1).

That's when everything changed. The butler told Pharaoh about Joseph's ability to interpret dreams. And the royal decree went forth to release him from prison. He quickly shaved and changed into white linen in order to stand before the king in proper Egyptian attire.

"I have heard it said of you that when you hear a dream you can interpret it," Pharaoh said inquisitively (41:15).

"I cannot do it," Joseph replied, "but God will give Pharaoh the answer he desires" (41:16).

Then Joseph proceeded to interpret Pharaoh's dreams about seven fat cows and seven lean cows as seven years of prosperity, followed by seven years of famine. Not only did Joseph give the monarch a glimpse into the future, but he proceeded to give him some administrative advice as well.

"And now," he suggested, "let Pharaoh look for a discerning and wise man and put him in charge of the land of Egypt" (41:33). Joseph further advised that they store a fifth (20 percent) of the annual harvest during the years of plenty. That would provide ample reserves for the years of famine in the future.

Pharaoh was so taken by Joseph's advice that he appointed him to become the grand vizier of Egypt. He would personally oversee this great administrative task of collecting, storing, and distributing the grain.

"Can we find anyone like this man, one in whom is the spirit of God?" Pharaoh asked. "There is no one so discerning and wise as you," he added. In one of history's dramatic reversals, Joseph went from the prison to the palace instantly. One cannot help but wonder what Potiphar and his wife must have thought!

Halftime

1. *Are you facing any situations in your life right now that seem impossible to resolve?*

2. *Is God the same today as He was in Joseph's time? Can He do the impossible for you as well?*

If Only They Could See Me Now

Everything changed overnight for Joseph. No more restless nights in the dungeon. He was sleeping in the palace. No more ragged clothes. He was dressed in royal robes, riding in the royal chariot. They even gave him an Egyptian name and an Egyptian wife (41:45). He was a big deal. If only his brothers could see him now!

Just as he had predicted, the seven years of plenty came. And they stored up so much grain they couldn't keep up with it all. But then the famine came as well. And Joseph sold the grain to the Egyptians, which increased Pharaoh's wealth all the more. Eventually people began coming from other countries to buy grain.

Joseph was now 37 years old. It had been 20 years since he had seen his family. But in all those tough times, God had not forgotten him. Neither had He forgotten the promise. In fact, if Joseph hadn't been in Egypt, all might have been lost. God was going to preserve the entire family through Joseph's provision.

The famine was so severe it reached Canaan as well (Genesis 42:1,2). And Jacob sent ten of his sons to Egypt to buy grain, but he kept Benjamin safely at home. When they arrived in Egypt, Joseph immediately recognized them. But they did not recognize him. He looked like an Egyptian, walked like an Egyptian, and talked like an Egyptian. So they naturally thought he was an Egyptian.

"Where do you come from?" he asked them harshly through an interpreter.

"From the land of Canaan," they replied, "to buy food."

"You are spies!" Joseph insisted.

"No!" they replied. "Your servants were twelve brothers, the sons of one man.... The youngest is now with our father, and one is no more," they added lamentably (42:13).

Joseph proceeded to tell them that one of them would have to remain behind as a hostage while the others returned to Canaan to get their younger brother.

"You must bring your youngest brother to me," Joseph insisted, wanting to see his brother.

Then the brothers turned to each other and said, "Surely we are being punished because of our brother." And they proceeded to discuss what they had done to Joseph and how guilty they felt.

All the time, Joseph was listening to every word they were saying. But he never let on that he understood them. Finally, he couldn't take it anymore and he began to weep. So he walked away.

Bad News and More Bad News

Joseph kept Simeon as the hostage. I've often wondered if he was the one who had been most hostile toward him. He certainly paid for it if he was. In the meantime, the other brothers set off for home. Their bags were loaded with grain, and their money was returned as well. But when they got back home without Simeon, Jacob threw a fit!

"You have deprived me of my children. Joseph is no more and Simeon is no more, and now you want to take Benjamin. Everything is against me!" (Genesis 42:36).

Now, on the surface of things, it may well have appeared that everything really was going *against* Jacob. But in reality, God was moving *for* Jacob. He was at work in every circumstance to accomplish His will and purpose in Jacob's life and in his entire family. It was all coming together like some grand masterpiece.

Reluctantly, Jacob finally agreed to let Benjamin return to Egypt with his other sons. It was a risky choice. This was Joseph's full brother. Rachel's other son. Jacob couldn't bear the thought of losing him too. But Judah spoke up and promised to personally guarantee his safety.

"God Almighty grant you mercy," Jacob said. "As for me, if I am bereaved, I am bereaved" (43:14). He had experienced so much pain that he abandoned himself and his family to God.

When they arrived in Egypt, Joseph was anxious to see them. But the sight of Benjamin was more than he could bear. Again, he ran out of the room and sobbed. When he returned, he tried to act tough with them again. But Judah begged him for mercy, even offering to be his personal slave if he would not harm Benjamin.

Judah begged Joseph, telling him what their father had said: "If you take this one from me too and harm comes to him, you will bring my gray head down to the grave in misery" (44:29). "He is so close to the boy, he'll die if we go back without him," Judah explained.

The Truth Comes Out

The grief they were all expressing was more than Joseph could bear. Finally, he burst into tears in front of them and told them who he was.

"I am Joseph! Is my father still living?" he asked.

They were absolutely terrified! All ten of them stood there in stunned silence.

Joseph! The prime minister of Egypt? The grand vizier of the whole land? Second only to Pharaoh? Oh, no!

"He's going to kill us!" they probably thought.

"Come close to me," he said. "I am your brother Joseph, the one you sold into Egypt! And now, do not be distressed...for selling me here, because it was to save lives that God sent me ahead of you...to preserve for you a remnant on earth and to save your lives by a great deliverance" (Genesis 45:4-7).

He explained the famine would last for seven whole years. Then he asked them to go home and insist that Jacob and the entire family move to Egypt to keep them alive.

"Tell him God has made me lord of all Egypt. Come quickly. Don't delay," Joseph insisted. Then he loaded them with provisions for the trip home. He sent a caravan of 20 donkeys and carts.

It must have been some meeting when the brothers had to tell their father that they had deceived him all those years.

"Joseph is still alive!" they announced. "In fact, he is ruler of all Egypt" (45:26).

Jacob was so stunned, he could not believe them at first. But as they unravelled their story, he realized it was true. And his spirit revived. Hope sprang anew in those old eyes. The deception was finally over. The deceiver was relieved. The truth was finally out.

"I'm convinced! My son Joseph is still alive," he shouted. "I will go and see him before I die" (45:28).

It was an incredible sight! They packed up their belongings, took down their tents, rounded up their cattle, and 70 of them pulled out of Beersheba, heading toward Egypt. Excitement and anticipation beat in every heart. The men, women, and children, who would become the nation of Israel, were headed to an appointment with destiny.

Jacob wasn't running for his life this time. He was riding in style. His son was the prime minister of Egypt. And he had an appointment with royalty to keep. He was going to meet the Pharaoh. But more than anything, he was going to see his beloved Joseph again face-to-face.

When Jacob arrived, Joseph threw his arms around his father and wept a long time. The son presumed dead was alive. Jacob was finally satisfied.

"Now I am ready to die," Jacob said. "I have seen you for myself."

What a great reunion it must have been. Not just of a father and a son, but of a whole family. And in that family the promise was kept alive.

All's Well That Ends Well

They settled in the fertile delta area in Lower (northern) Egypt. There they prospered and multiplied in the years to come. God had reversed the brothers' hostility into blessing. He had overruled their wickedness and made Joseph ruler of Egypt.

Several years later, Jacob died at a good old age. And Joseph had the body embalmed. Then a royal procession carried his mummified remains back to Canaan to the burial place of Abraham and Isaac. Jacob's wanderings were over. He was finally coming home. And what a homecoming it was!

God is still in the business of happy endings. He still takes shattered lives and rebuilds them to His glory. Remember Bob at the beginning of the chapter? God sustained him through the divorce and the separation from his children. He later remarried and committed his life to full-time service. Today, he is one of the nation's leading ministers to singles. And his marriage is a model of Christian love and devotion.

> *God is still in the business of happy endings. He still takes shattered lives and rebuilds them to His glory.*

You may feel that your life has been shattered by some personal crisis. But God can still turn it all around to His glory. Trust Him! He's already in the process of working it out.

Postgame Highlights

1. *Are there any conflicts in your family that need to be resolved?*

2. *What steps might God want you to take to help resolve them?*

3. *If you were to look back over your life, what would you have done differently?*

Personal Interview

List those times when God did the impossible for you. And trust Him to do it again!

_____

_____

_____

Final Wrap-up

Faith is the art of holding on to things in spite of your changing moods and circumstances.

—C.S. Lewis

CHAPTER

4

Becoming a Leader:

Overcoming Your Past

Everyone fails sooner or later. Failure is a normal part of human life. There are things back there on the road of life that we would just as soon leave behind: wrong choices, wrong actions, sins, fears, mistakes, disappointments, and heartaches.

Failure is especially hard on leaders. We don't want to fail. In fact, we fear failure because we've seen what it does to people. And as for all those little talks about learning from our failures—forget it! We don't want any part of it. But then it happens! We find ourselves face-to-face with failure and with ourselves.

That is the hardest part of dealing with failure—dealing with ourselves. It is so hard for us to face failure, especially as men. We don't want to fail. We don't want to admit we've failed. We don't want to do anything about it.

That's where God comes in. He turns failures into leaders. Take Moses, for example.

The Book of Exodus tells us that the Israelites prospered in Egypt, even after the deaths of Jacob and Joseph. But as time passed, a problem arose. The Bible explains: "Then a new king, who did not know about Joseph, came to power in Egypt" (Exodus 1:8). That was the beginning of trouble. There was a new CEO, if you will. And he didn't know about all the good work of the previous managers and employees. So he started cleaning house on the corporate structure.

Actually, a whole new dynasty of Pharaohs came to power. All the previous policies were revoked. And the Israelites became the target of many of those changes. Many scholars believe these newcomers were the Hyksos—outsiders who briefly ruled Egypt. That would explain why they were concerned about the Israelites becoming too numerous for them.

So the new pharaoh oppressed the Israelites and enslaved them. He reduced them to forced labor: field hands, brick makers, builders. But the Israelites continued to multiply. Next, the Pharaoh ordered the Hebrew midwives to kill all the newborn male babies. When they refused, he ordered the Egyptians to throw the babies into the Nile River. It was into this desperate situation that Moses was born many years later.

Desperate Times Call for Desperate Measures

A couple from the tribe of Levi (the family of priests) had a baby boy. Not wanting him to die, they hid him for three months. Finally, in desperation, the mother made a papyrus basket, coated it with tar, put the baby inside, and set him among the papyrus reeds (KJV, "bulrushes") in the Nile River. In desperation, she did what she felt she had to do. She abandoned him to God.

In the meantime, Pharaoh's daughter came down to the river to bathe and found the basket. We've all heard the story of "Moses and the Bulrushes" ever since we were lit-tle kids. When I was young, I mistakenly called it "Moses and the Bulldozers." At any rate, here is a child born into poverty and slavery, discovered by Pharaoh's daughter, and raised as her own son in wealth and splendor.

Since the Egyptians considered the Nile River to be a god, the princess took the child to be a gift from god (probably Hapi, the "spirit" of the Nile). Her heart was moved by the baby's cries. She "adopted" him as her own son and named him Moses after the royal throne name of the Pharaoh (Thut*mosis*). There can be little doubt that she hoped her son would rule Egypt one day as the new Pharaoh.

Perhaps you have read the debate in the newspapers about who is going to ascend the throne of England next. Will this one or that one be king? And what about the queen? We Americans can hardly imagine the intense anx-iety of ancient royal families over who would be the next ruler. It consumed the royal family for years. The princess's dream was to see her son on the throne.

Moses had the finest education, military training, and social training that money could buy. He looked like an Egyptian. He walked like an Egyptian. And he talked like an Egyptian. But his heart was with the people of Israel. When he saw an Egyptian beating a Hebrew one day, he couldn't restrain himself. He tried to intervene and inad-vertently killed the Egyptian. It was an offense punishable by death, even for a member of the royal family.

Moses, who had spent years living in prosperity in the palace, ended up running for his life. He fled from Pharaoh into the wilderness of Sinai and came to the outpost of Midian. And there he remained for 40 years. The man born in poverty, raised in prosperity, now ended up living in obscurity on the back side of the desert. It was almost as though God had failed him and given up on him. But in reality, God was preparing him for an even greater and more effective ministry in the future.

If there was ever a time when the promise seemed to fade, it was during those long difficult years in the desert. All hope seemed lost. The Israelites were in bondage. Moses was in exile. And God was silent.

But all was not lost. God had not abandoned His people. Exodus 2:24,25 says, "God heard their groaning and he remembered his covenant....So God looked on the Israelites and was concerned about them." Three things were happening while it seemed nothing was happening:

1. God heard.
2. God remembered.
3. God looked.

And then, God called!

Time Out

1. Do you feel like God has forsaken you? Or that He can't use you?

2. What is He trying to teach you right now?

Learning from Your Mistakes

Every time I read the story of Moses, I am reminded that it really doesn't matter what your background is. You can either benefit from it, or you can rise above it. You may come from a very prosperous background. For some it is a blessing. For others it is a curse.

You may come from a very poor background. You may have had to learn to make your own way in life. And rise above your circumstances. I come from a long line of truck drivers. My father was a truck driver. My uncles were all truck drivers. My grandfather was a truck driver. And my great-grandfather drove wagons. As far back as anybody can remember, all the men in our family were truck drivers.

My dad dropped out of school in the ninth grade. My mother dropped out in the tenth grade. I grew up in an uneducated family. Today, I have seven earned degrees. People often ask me, "Don't you have enough education yet?" I answer, "I'm trying to make up for my family background." But

It really doesn't matter what your background is. You can either benefit from it, or you can rise above it.

one of the things I have observed in my life is this: Because I grew up in a truck driver's home, I never became so educated that I lost touch with the average man. All we spoke in our family was "truck driver" English: "Where's the food? What's for dinner? Hurry up!" That sort of thing.

God will always use your background, even with its limitations, to prepare you for whatever it is that He wants you to do in life. I believe God has called me to communicate His Word to average people in a way that they can understand it and grow to love it. And that means in spite of my education. I appreciate the education I received. But I still talk like an ordinary person, in spite of my education, because that's how I was raised.

It doesn't matter what your background is. Look at Moses, the son of a slave. His bed was a basket adrift on the Nile River. He was picked up by Pharaoh's daughter and raised in a palace with the greatest luxury of his time. Now he ends up out in the middle of the desert in total obscurity.

Born into slavery.
Raised in luxury.
Lost in obscurity.

A Second Chance

After 40 years of keeping the flock of his father-in-law on the back side of the desert, Moses met with God. He came to Mount Sinai, and on the side of the mountain he saw a bush burning and blazing with fire. And it continued to burn but was not burned up.

The burning bush caught his attention so dramatically that he said, "I'm going to turn aside and see this great sight. This bush that is on fire and is not consumed!" It is not unusual for a bush with a high phosphorous content to catch on fire in the desert. But ultimately it would burn up and burn out. This bush kept burning, and burning, and burning because it was glowing with the very presence of God. The *shekinah* glory of the Almighty had settled there.

Moses didn't realize what it was. So he hiked up onto the mountain to get a closer look at this unusual sight. And the Bible tells us the angel of the Lord appeared to him out of the flame of fire in the midst of the burning bush. He said to Moses, "Take off your sandals, for the place where you are standing is holy ground.... I am the God of your father, the God of Abraham, the God of Isaac and the God of Jacob" (Exodus 3:5,6).

Then God explained what He had been doing all that time. "I have indeed seen... I have heard... and I am concerned... so I have come down to rescue them" (3:7,8). That was good news to Moses' ears. But what came next shocked him senseless.

"So now, go. I am sending you to Pharaoh to bring my people the Israelites out of Egypt," God told him (3:10).

Forty years earlier he had run ahead of God. Now he hesitated to move at all. Then the excuses began flowing:

1. *Inadequate.* "Who am I, that I should go to Pharaoh?" (3:11).
2. *Ignorant.* "What shall I tell them?" (3:13).
3. *Insecure.* "What if they do not believe me?" (4:1).

4. *Inferior.* "I have never been eloquent.... I am slow of speech and tongue" (4:10).
5. *Insufficient.* "O Lord, please send someone else to do it" (4:13).

When God Takes Over

Finally, Moses gave up and listened.

God said to him, "Say to the Israelites: 'I AM has sent me'" (Exodus 3:14). "The God who always was, who always is, and who always will be. The God who is eternally present. The great self-existing God. I AM. That is the name you can use. And they'll know who I am. I AM the One who can help them. I AM the Promisor."

Moses' excuses are not unlike our own. God may have tugged at your heart and said, "I want you to teach Sunday school, serve as a deacon or an elder (or in some other position of leadership) in your church." And you said, "You've got the wrong guy! I can't do that! Look at all my other responsibilities. Find somebody else!"

That's what Moses said. "I can't do it! Why, who would take care of the sheep? Besides, I'm a wanted man back in Egypt!"

But God said, "They've forgotten who you are!"

"Besides that, I'm not eloquent," Moses protested.

God's reply was, "Who gave man his mouth? Who makes him deaf or dumb?...Is it not I?" (4:11). In other words, "If you have what you think is a limitation, could I remind you, Moses, I am the God who made people. And I am the God who made you with your limitation. I want to use you despite your limitation so that you will bring glory to Me. I will be your mouth, and I will put the words in your mouth to let you know what to say. Besides that, if you need help, go back to Egypt and find your brother Aaron. He can speak for you."

God took away every excuse Moses had. When Moses finally went back to Egypt, he let Aaron speak only one time. And he did such a terrible job that Moses never let him talk again. From that point on, Moses did all of his own talking. Moses finally returned to Egypt—out of obscurity, into adversity, and on to victory.

No One Said It Would Be Easy

It is not easy for leaders to come back. First, because we expect so much of them. Second, because they expect so much of themselves. But Moses had been fully prepared and equipped by his past. He was the only Israelite who had ever walked into the royal palace before. He was the only one familiar with Egyptian royalty. He was certainly the right man for the job.

Moses was also prepared because he had failed. He had tasted the bitter fruit of disappointment. And he knew what a second chance really meant. It meant a whole new life. A chance to redeem the moment and to right the wrong that had been done.

It is not easy for leaders to come back. First, because we expect so much of them. Second, because they expect so much of themselves.

Many of us have been there. I certainly have. One moment we have so much, and then it's gone! You're in the desert, on the bench, or in the penalty box—alone...with God. And that is when He becomes so real to us. When it's just you and God. When there's nobody else to lean on. When all the props are removed. That's when faith is put to the ultimate test.

In those lonely moments we are forced to reexamine ourselves—our beliefs, our values, and our future. We begin to realize what really matters most in life: our relationship to God and our relationship to our family. Everything else is secondary. Yet, in the success of life, it is easy to forget that. To neglect and overlook that which really means the most to you.

While you are standing in the desert, you are consumed by the enormity of it. A seemingly vast wilderness of empty space. And yet, even in the desert, there is life. There is survival. And there is God. Ready to meet you at your lowest and loneliest point. Ready to ask, "What is that in your hand?" You see, the answer is always closer than we think.

Halftime

1. Is our situation ever really totally hopeless?

2. Are you in the desert of life right now? Look around. Where is God?

Back to the Beginning

The journey back to Egypt was long and hard. Moses had plenty of time to think it all over. He even had some close calls along the way. But there was no turning back now. He had made his decision. He was going to be a leader!

Moses and Aaron gathered the elders of Israel together and explained to them what God had said He would do for them. Their response was positive. The Bible says, "And they believed" (Exodus 4:31). Their renewed faith triggered a hope for the future.

Then the Scripture adds this further note: "When they heard that the LORD was concerned about them...they bowed down and worshiped." When people are convinced that God cares about them, they cannot help but fall at His feet and worship Him. Faith, worship, hope—these were the keys to their success.

Moses was ready now to face his past. He went to Pharaoh with a tremendous sense of courage because he had met God face-to-face. No fear. No hesitation. He simply said, "Let my people go!" To which Pharaoh in essence said, "You're out of your mind! Get rid of this free source of labor? Are you crazy? No way!"

God never said being a leader would be easy. But Moses was undeterred by the king's resistance. Initially, Moses asked only that they be allowed to go out in the desert to worship God for three days and come back. Later he would ask permission for the Israelites to leave and never return. But God had to prepare the way for that to happen.

They had to go through a whole series of confrontations involving plagues of lice and frogs and flies and bugs and everything you can imagine. Some were tragic. Some were almost hilarious. The houses filled up with frogs in one of the plagues. And the Bible says there were frogs in their beds, in their ovens, and on their floors. They multiplied by the millions! And the Egyptians could not get rid of them.

Moses came to see Pharaoh and said, "How do you like these frogs?"

Pharaoh said, "I don't like them! Get rid of them!"

"Let my people go!" Moses insisted.

"You may go," Pharaoh agreed.

Then Moses asked Pharaoh, "When do you want me to get rid of the frogs?"

And Pharaoh said, "Tomorrow!"

Why didn't he say, "Right now"? Was it because he wanted to spend one more night at home with the frogs? No, when he said tomorrow, he meant as soon as possible.

Each plague was aimed at the gods of Egypt. Each was designed to convince the Pharaoh that the Lord was superior to their idols and false gods. There were ten plagues in all.

1. Nile to blood versus Hapi and Osiris (Nile gods)
2. Frogs versus Heqt (frog goddess)
3. Beetles versus Khepra (divine scarab)
4. Flies versus Uatchit (fly god)
5. Livestock versus Apis and Hathor (cow gods)
6. Boils versus Imhotep (divine healer)
7. Hail versus Qetesh (storm god)
8. Locusts versus Isis (goddess of fertility)
9. Darkness versus Ra (sun god)
10. Death versus Ptah (god of life)

Moses went through all these confrontations. Pharaoh changed his mind time after time. "You can go....No, you can't go." What he was really saying was, "I'm not really sure this is the hand of God. Maybe it's just a coincidental circumstance, a quirk of nature, or some other such thing." But the last two plagues struck at the very heart of Egyptian religion: the sun and the sons. In a desert kingdom, everything revolved around the sun. So the plague of darkness frightened them to death. And in every ancient society, no one was more important than the firstborn son. Especially the son of Pharaoh. He was the god incarnate, destined for the throne. To the Egyptians, his death meant the death of God.

Finally, Moses warned Pharaoh, "If you don't let us go, the firstborn of every child in Egypt will die, including Pharaoh's own son." On that night, the death angel passed over Egypt—and the firstborn of every Egyptian family died, including Pharaoh's son. He was so brokenhearted he finally said, "Go, and never come back!"

The Price of Leadership

Moses had confronted the greatest and most powerful ruler in the ancient world. And he had won! He had not only conquered Pharaoh, but he had also conquered himself and his past. No more wallowing in his guilt and failure.

He had won! No more wishing he were the Pharaoh. He had defeated the Pharaoh.

But that was just the beginning of the long road of leadership. He had to lead these former slaves to the Promised Land. However, they weren't used to all that freedom. So there were some real bumps in the road ahead.

But one thing was clear as they marched out of Egypt: The promise was alive! It had lain dormant for many years, but it had not died. The Promisor was still alive! Psalm 105:42,43 says: "For he remembered his holy promise.... He brought out his people with rejoicing, his chosen ones with shouts of joy."

Real leaders don't quit when the road gets rough. They move ahead and march off the map!

The Israelites got out of town with relative ease. They even took Joseph's mummy with them. But when they turned south toward the Red Sea, they found themselves in a bind. They were trapped by the water when Pharaoh changed his mind and sent his army after them. Six hundred chariots appeared on the horizon. That's when the Israelites turned on Moses. They began to imply, "What kind of leader are you? You brought us out here to the edge of the Red Sea. And we're all going to get killed! We should have stayed back in Egypt."

Moses began to pay the price of leadership. It was difficult enough dealing with the Egyptians. Now he had to deal with his own people as well. But this was certainly no time to turn back. Real leaders don't quit when the road gets rough. They move ahead and march off the map!

"Stand firm," Moses told the Israelites, "and you will see the deliverance (KJV, "salvation") the LORD will bring you today" (Exodus 14:13). The Bible tells us he raised his rod, and God sent a great east wind (a desert sandstorm) to split the waters of the Red Sea. And the Israelites went across on the dry land. Then the waters closed up on Pharaoh's army and destroyed it. Pharaoh was defeated. His army was drowned. And the children of Israel were delivered on the other side.

But that was not the end of the story. Moses continued to lead the people in the Sinai wilderness. He had defeated Pharaoh. He had crossed the Red Sea. But when he got into the wilderness, he had to contend with his own people. It's sort of like the pastor who said to me one time, "I really enjoy everything about the ministry except the people. They're just so hard to get along with!" That's when real leadership begins.

Moses had led them to an incredible victory, but it didn't seem to matter. They got into the wilderness and said, "There's nothing to drink here." So God brought water from a rock. "There's nothing to eat here." So God brought manna from heaven. "We don't like manna. We want meat." So God brought quail. Then they said they were sick of quail. Finally, there was open rebellion. So God opened up the earth, and it swallowed part of them. The rest of them finally got the point. They were supposed to follow God's man to God's destination.

Despite all the difficulties, it was there in that wilderness that God's greatest blessings came. There they received the Law and the Ten Commandments. There they built the Tabernacle. There they established a place to worship God. It was there in the wilderness that the glory of God came down from heaven and rested on the ark of the covenant in the holy of holies in the Tabernacle.

It took 40 long years in the wilderness to learn the lessons God needed to teach them. But eventually Moses brought them to the place of victory. You may be going through a tough time in your life right now. You may feel like you are in the wilderness. Perhaps the struggle has been long and difficult. You don't know when you're ever going to see the light at the end of the tunnel. Friend, God is still there every step of the way. In the times of difficulty as well as the times of blessing, He has not forgotten you.

Learning from the Wilderness

When I turned 40, I went through one of those wilderness times in my life. For ten years I had taught the largest adult Bible class in America to over 3,000 people every week. It was the joy and thrill of my life. Like many younger men, I thought it would last forever. But one day all that vanished! What hurt most is that the situation was my own fault.

The months that followed were difficult and painful. I sought God's direction, but it did not come. I wanted Him to work it out for me. But He wanted to work on me. Time passed. I kept insisting, but God kept waiting. Though I didn't realize it at the time, He was working on me so that I would be ready when the call came.

After nearly two years, God opened a wonderful door of opportunity for our family. It meant a lot of changes. A move. A new town. New people. A new church. And new responsibilities. Among them, I was asked to teach an adult Bible class. On the first Sunday, 11 people showed up, including my wife and the pastor's wife. She came just to encourage us.

Yet it was a new beginning, and I loved it! Suddenly, my pain was gone. It was just as thrilling to teach those 11 people as it was to teach 3,000. The desert began to blossom. And soon the 11 grew to several hundred. Today, our ministry again touches thousands.

You may be at one of those wilderness points in your life. Don't give up! And whatever you do, don't blame God. He is there with you every step of the way. Even when he is silent. Remember what He was doing while the Israelites were in bondage? He *saw* their plight. He *heard* their cries. He *remembered* His promises. And He *came* to rescue them. And He will rescue you, too—when He is finished preparing you.

When failure comes your way, remember:

1. *To fail is to be fully human.* God is fully aware of your limitations. True success is not avoiding failure but learning what to do with it.
2. *To fail is not to be a failure.* Babe Ruth is remembered for his home runs. But he also set the record for the most strike-outs.
3. *No one is a failure until he stops trying.* Thomas Edison made over 5,000 attempts before he finally invented a light bulb that worked.
4. *Failure is never final if you get up one more time than you fall down.* The fear of failure is far greater than the failure itself. If you've failed, admit it and start over. Focus on your future, not your past.

Perhaps things haven't gone well. And you are in obscurity for now. This is not the end. It is only the process. It will lead to greater things. You may have lost a position of leadership, been demoted to another job, taken a pay cut—or all of the above!

Perhaps everything is going great right now. You may be riding the wave of success. Could I remind you: When you're *up*, have a heart for those who are *down*. Reach down and lift them up. So that when they're up and you're down, they can reach down and lift you up as well. Believe it or not, most of us can survive failure. The greatest temptation of all is dealing with success.

Moses is an incredible example for us. Born in poverty. Raised in prosperity. Sent into obscurity. Brought back in victory. What made the difference? He met God in the wilderness. After the burning bush, he knew that he was no longer alone. God was with him. And God made all the difference. And He has promised to do the same for you.

Postgame Highlights

1. *What is the greatest lesson God is teaching you right now?*

2. *Are you learning it?*

3. *What improvements do you still need to make?*

Personal Interview

If you are going to be successful as a leader, what is it you are going to have to overcome?

_____

_____

_____

_____

Final Wrap-up

My great concern is not whether you have failed, but whether you are content with your failure.

—Abraham Lincoln

Success in the Battle:

Conquering the Opposition

Life has its ups and downs. For many people it is an ongoing battle. A conflict of values. A battle of beliefs. A struggle of wills. A war of nerves. God never promised this life would be easy. But He does promise to go with us through every conflict.

After Moses' death, God called Joshua to lead the army of Israel into the Promised Land. They had been in the Sinai wilderness for 40 years. The older generation had died in the wilderness, and the younger generation was ready to move ahead.

"Be strong and courageous," God commanded Joshua. "Do not let this Book of the Law depart from your mouth; meditate on it day and night...then you will be prosperous and successful. Have I not commanded you? Be strong and courageous" (Joshua 1:8,9).

Prosperity and success. Those are pretty big promises. God was telling Joshua to put Him first, and then he would be prosperous and successful. Most men either miss this point altogether or get it backward. They put prosperity and success first. It becomes their all-consuming goal. Then, if they have time, they get around to God last.

"Honey, once we get some financial security, I'll start going to church." How many wives have heard that same excuse again and again? "Just give me time to learn this new job, then I'll have time for God." But it never happens. There never is time for God because your priorities are out of order. God isn't first. And in some cases, He isn't even on the list!

Joshua knew he was facing incredible odds. He was trying to lead a band of former slaves against the fortified cities of Canaan. The walls looked insurmountable. The people appeared unconquerable. But God promised, and that was the key. The promise meant everything, which included conquering the land God had promised to Abraham, Isaac, Jacob, and their descendants.

Joshua placed the challenge in front of the men of Israel. And they replied, "Whatever you have commanded us we will do, and wherever you send us we will go" (Joshua 1:16). In fact, they even made a pact to execute anyone who rebelled against his orders. They were "burning their bridges" behind them. There was no turning back now.

"Only be strong and courageous!" the men shouted. These were the young men whose parents died because of disobedience in the wilderness. They had seen firsthand what cowardice could do, and they wanted no part of it. They couldn't go back now. So they were determined to go on to victory.

Check Out Your Options

Before they charged ahead to attack Jericho, Joshua sent two spies to check it out. Two may not seem like much, but Joshua had been part of the contingent of 12 spies that Moses had sent out 40 years earlier. Remember, only 2 of the 12, Joshua and Caleb, brought back a positive report. The other ten were overwhelmed with fear and convinced the Israelites to turn back into the wilderness.

He wasn't about to make that mistake again. So he sent only two spies. When they got to Jericho, they discovered it to be one of the great walled cities of the ancient world. It sat on an artificial mound, already several centuries old. Its massive double walls surrounded the tell (or mound). An imposing site to the desert spies.

When you check out the options in life, it doesn't take long to realize that God has the best deal to offer

Jericho sat near where the Jordan River drops into the Dead Sea. It literally guarded the entrance into Canaan from the wilderness. But when the spies arrived, they found the city already in panic over the advancing Israelites. The people of Jericho were scared to death because they had heard that God was with them.

Now, the Israelites didn't have a superior army. They weren't even well trained. They had very limited military experience. And they didn't even have a battle plan. But God was with them, and that is all that mattered. The spies rushed back with the good news: "Jericho is afraid of our God."

When you check out the options in life, it doesn't take long to realize that God has the best deal to offer. All other options are empty and meaningless by comparison. When you realize what you have in Christ, you realize He is all you need. Everything else pales in comparison.

Step Out on Faith

It was time to take a serious step of faith–across the Jordan River. "Consecrate yourselves," Joshua told the men of Israel. "Take up the ark of the covenant," he ordered the priests, "and cross over ahead of the people" (Joshua 3:5,6). The ark was the symbol of God's presence. His glory rested inside this golden chest. Carrying the ark in front of the people symbolized that they were following God's lead.

Joshua instructed the priests to carry the ark of the covenant to the river's edge and step into the water. However, there was a problem with this instruction. The Jordan River was flooded from the spring rains.

"Don't worry," Joshua explained. "The water will part miraculously."

Just as God had parted the Red Sea for Moses, He was going to part the waters of the Jordan for Joshua. Sure enough, as soon as the priests stepped into the water, it stopped flowing downstream. The water was dammed up several miles north at the town of Adam (Joshua 3:16). Since the river drops in elevation as it flows southward, the remaining water simply flowed down into the Dead Sea. And the Israelites crossed over on dry ground.

You can stand on the mound at Jericho today and see the Jordan River in the distance. This means that the Canaanites at Jericho certainly saw the waters part. They had to be shocked. The God of Israel who parted the Red Sea had now parted the Jordan before their very eyes. Who could stand against Him?

Perhaps you are hesitating to take a step of faith in your life. Could I remind you that the same God who stood by Joshua will stand by you. He will go with you all the way. He never asks you to do anything that He will not make possible for you to do. Take that step of obedience and surrender to Him right now.

Imagine the excitement of those Israelites. They had seen a miracle of God! Right before their eyes. Some of them were small children when they crossed the Red Sea years earlier. But most of them had been born since then in the wilderness. They had never seen anything like this before. They were excited and ready to charge on to Jericho.

Did We Forget Something?

As usual, God had another idea. He told them to camp at Gilgal. "Make flint knives," he told Joshua, "and circumcise the Israelites" (Joshua 5:2). What? That's no way to get these men ready for battle. I can just imagine their reaction. "You want to do what! Are you crazy? Here? Now?"

Circumcision, remember, was the sign of their covenant with God. All males were to be circumcised eight days after their birth. So why were they doing this now? The Bible explains that all of the men who came out of Egypt in the exodus had already been circumcised. But all of the boys born in the wilderness had not been circumcised.

How could they have neglected something so important to God's people? Do you remember what went wrong in the wilderness? They crossed the Sinai desert in about two months. But when the spies brought the negative report from Canaan, the people turned back in disbelief. Then, God made them wander around the desert for 40 years.

They had disobeyed God, and God would not let them go into the Promised Land until that generation died in the

If we don't obey God in our generation, He will skip over our generation and move on to the next generation that will trust Him.

wilderness. There is no other explanation for what happened. God must not have allowed them to circumcise and dedicate their children to Him. "If you are not going to obey Me, then don't make a mockery of dedicating your children to Me."

They had lost sight of the promise. They wandered in unbelief until that generation of doubters was gone. There is a powerful principle in this story—a principle that convicts the heart of every adult. If we don't obey God in our generation, He will skip over our generation and move on to the next generation that will trust Him.

Time Out

1. Am I really being the example to my children that they need and deserve?

2. What changes and improvements do I need to make?

Let God Take Over

The Israelites had plenty of time to think things over while they recuperated at Gilgal. Ironically, the name of the place means "rolling." It was there that they rolled away the flesh of their foreskins. "Today I have rolled away the reproach of Egypt from you," God explained (Joshua 5:9). And they each got the point!

They also celebrated the Passover at Gilgal—the first one to be celebrated in the Promised Land. After that, the manna stopped appearing. God finally had His army ready. But notice, He did it His way. There was nothing to depend on but Him.

In the meantime, Joshua must have wondered how he would ever be able to take Jericho. He didn't have a battle plan, so he strolled over the hills to get a better look at Jericho. En route, he met a man with a drawn sword in his hand.

"Are you for us or for our enemies?" Joshua asked.

"Neither," he replied, "but as commander of the army of the LORD I have now come" (5:13,14).

Joshua fell on his face before Him. It was the angel of the Lord, Christ Himself—the Captain of the heavenly host. When Joshua, whose name means "savior," realized that he was standing before the Savior, he immediately fell down before Him.

The appearances of Christ in the Old Testament are called "Christophanies." They are temporary appearances of the Savior prior to His permanent incarnation as Jesus. They only occur on special occasions. This was one of those occasions.

"Take off your sandals," the Savior said, "for the place where you are standing is holy" (Joshua 5:15).

A savior meets the Savior! Joshua was standing on holy ground just like Moses did at the burning bush. Barefoot before God with his feet in the sand, Joshua was reminded that all men are nothing more than dust before the Almighty.

God's Battle Plan

Then, God gave Joshua His battle plan. "March around the city once with all the armed men. Do this for six days. Have seven priests carry trumpets of rams' horns in front of the ark. On the seventh day, march around the city seven times blowing the trumpets.... Have all the people give a loud shout; then the wall of the city will collapse" (6:3-5).

Joshua did not argue. He did not hesitate. He obeyed God. One of the great character strengths of his life was his confidence in God. It was the source of his courage. It was the key to his success.

Imagine being a Canaanite at Jericho. The city is ready. The walls are up. The gates are barred. The soldiers are positioned. Their swords and spears are in their hands. They're waiting for the Israelites. And finally they appear!

"Here they come!" the shout goes up.

The dust rises on the desert. The Canaanites see this host marching toward Jericho. They get ready—shields up, spears up. But all the Israelites do is march around the walls carrying a golden box. And after one complete circle they leave, marching back over the horizon to Gilgal.

"They chickened out!" they may have said. "Must be afraid of us! Yeah, we're tough—real tough!"

But the next day the Israelites came back. "Get ready! Here they come again."

Again, they just marched around the city, blowing their trumpets and carrying that golden box. Then they marched off again.

By the sixth day it had become ridiculous. Perhaps the Canaanites taunted them: "Here they come again! There they go again! Cowards!"

But on the seventh day, things changed. This time the Israelites kept on circling the city walls. Again. And again. And again. Seven times. As the psychological pressure built to a crescendo on the seventh time, they stopped and blew their trumpets louder than before. Then they shouted, and God moved.

The walls began to crack. The embankment caved in. The ground shook. The inner wall collapsed and tumbled down the mound, covering the outer wall with broken bricks. The stone wall began to break away. And the Canaanites themselves cracked up!

As the walls fell down, the Canaanites fled into the city. The Israelites climbed up over the rubble and captured the city. They destroyed it and burned it to the ground. The layer of ashes and the pile of bricks from that day are still there in the excavation.

God won a great victory that day for His people. The greatest and oldest city of Canaan had crumbled before the God of Israel. It wasn't long before the entire nation of Canaan had fallen. As you read the Book of Joshua, with the exception of one minor setback at Ai, the Israelites won victory after victory because God went with them.

The Israelites stepped out on faith. They sanctified their hearts and bodies. They submitted to the Lord. And they found the success He promised. In a few short years, the land—Israel, the Promised Land—was theirs.

Halftime

1. *Am I winning or losing at life?*

2. *What changes would I have to make to be victorious?*

Looking Back and Looking Ahead

There is nothing more satisfying than being able to look back over a job well done, whether it's mowing the lawn, painting the house, or fixing the car. There's just something fulfilling about getting the job done and doing it right.

Joshua conquered Canaan section by section: central, southern, and northern. In all, 31 cities fell to his army. Israel's borders stretched from the Sinai to Lebanon and from the Mediterranean to the East Bank of the Jordan. Next, they divided the land among the 12 tribes of Israel, and settled down to plant the new nation.

Before Joshua died, he gathered the tribes together at Shechem and gave his farewell address (Joshua 24). He reminded them that God had called Abraham from the land "beyond the River," and that He had promised to give this land to Isaac, Jacob, and their descendants. Next, he reminded them that God had called Moses to lead them out of Egypt. Finally, Joshua reminded them that it was God who fought for them in the conquest of Canaan.

Joshua wisely took the people back over their history. Each lesson was intended to reinforce their faith in God, who had kept the promise alive all those years. Now it was up to them to settle this land to His glory and to build a nation that would honor Him.

"Now fear the LORD and serve him with all faithfulness," Joshua urged them. "Throw away the gods your forefathers worshiped beyond the River and in Egypt, and serve the LORD" (verse 14). He was reminding them that Abraham had forsaken the gods of Babylon, and that they had been delivered from the gods of the Egyptians. Surely they wouldn't serve the gods of the Amorites and Canaanites whom they had just conquered!

Even today, many men fear surrendering their lives to God. But the truth is that such surrender brings life's greatest victories.

Then Joshua made an unusual request: "But if serving the LORD seems undesirable to you, then choose for yourselves this day whom you will serve" (verse 15). He left no doubt in their minds what their options were. They could worship the gods of Babylon, Egypt, or Canaan, or they could worship the Lord—the true and living God.

This may sound like a strange request under the circumstances, but Joshua knew the days of conflict were over. Now they would be tempted to be "at ease in Zion." Sometimes, when everything is going well, we fall the farthest away from God. Our need for Him is not as great, so our prayers to Him are not as fervent. Suddenly, without notice, we've slipped away from Him.

Even today, many men fear surrendering their lives to God. They think they are going to lose out on something or that it's going to cost them too much. But the truth is that such surrender brings life's greatest victories. If you are not serving God, you're serving someone. If you are not living for God, you're living for yourself or for the devil!

The three options had to sound ridiculous to the Israelites. Who would want to go back to the gods of the Babylonians? They left them years before. And the gods of the Egyptians who put us in bondage? No way! And as for the gods of the Amorites and Canaanites—Baal and Ashtar? We just conquered them!

As for Me and My House

Somehow Joshua knew this issue would face them again in the future. "But as for me and my household," he declared, "we will serve the LORD" (verse 15).

The people responded to the challenge. "We too will serve the Lord," they said, "because he is our God" (verse 18). They renounced the gods of Babylon, Egypt, and Canaan and pledged their faith in the Lord.

Then Joshua reminded them, "You are witnesses against yourselves that you have chosen to serve the LORD" (verse 22).

"Yes, we are witnesses," the people replied.

Once again, it was a high and holy day. A new nation was born on that day in the Promised Land. The covenant with God was renewed (verse 25), and the people of that generation kept their promise to God. The Bible records: "Israel served the LORD throughout the lifetime of Joshua and of the elders who outlived him and who had experienced everything the LORD had done for Israel" (verse 31).

Then they buried Joseph's body at Shechem in the soil of the Promised Land. They had carried his mummified body with them from Egypt. He was finally home, back in the land from which he had been sent away by his own brothers. Finally, after 400 years, he had come home. God had kept the promise!

As time passed, there would be new struggles and new challenges. Later generations would turn away from God and follow the gods of the defeated Canaanites. They would try to coexist with the enemy, only to be corrupted and defeated by them.

But for Joshua's generation, there was total victory. They had already seen what defeat was like in the wilderness, and they refused to go back. Realizing they had only one real choice, they marched ahead to victory. And what a glorious victory it was!

Going All the Way

Halfhearted commitments never really work. Bill Jackson tried to live that way for years. He would attend church regularly if nothing more important came up. After all, that was a real sacrifice for him. It meant giving up golf on Sundays. It even meant getting to bed at a decent time on Saturday nights.

"God ought to be glad I'm here as much as I am," Bill used to tell everyone. "I'm doing a whole lot better than most guys."

The problem was, Bill wasn't really doing well at all. His life was as up and down as a spastic yo-yo. Everything was out of balance, and almost everything was out of control. What's more, he wasn't happy or satisfied at all.

"It doesn't really work," he told me one day.

"What doesn't work?" I asked.

"The Christian life!" he replied. "It's really not what it's supposed to be."

"You mean you're not satisfied?" I asked.

"Not at all!" he insisted.

"Have you ever wondered if God is not satisfied with you?" I asked, peering into his eyes.

Bill dropped his head. "I'm sure He's not," he admitted.

"Maybe that's why you're not satisfied either," I suggested.

Then Bill looked at me as if he was finally ready to listen, like he really wanted to know how to make it better.

As we talked, I explained that halfhearted Christianity never does work. It's just enough religion to make us miserable. We know we can't go back into the world; there's no satisfaction in spiritual bondage. But if we don't go on to victory, we are destined to remain stuck in a vast spiritual wilderness.

It's like being stuck on a fence," I explained. "You've come far enough to know you need to go on. But if you don't get off that fence, you'll never be happy. And you sure won't be comfortable!"

Bill paused for a moment. I could see him struggling within. Then in a moment of complete honesty, he said, "If I go all the way with God, it's really going to cost me."

"No it isn't!" I responded. "It's going to cost you if you don't go all the way!"

In the weeks that followed, Bill wrestled with God's claims on his life. Even when we didn't talk about it, I could still see the struggle on his face. Some people come to grips with the decision for total commitment fairly easily. But for others, it is a real struggle, and we don't dare shortcut that process. It's like giving birth to a baby. You can't rush it. But when it's time, it comes.

One day Bill dropped in to see me unannounced. He had a serious look on his face as he sat down. Yet, there was also a sense of anticipation about him.

"You're right," he said.

"About what?" I asked.

"About being on the fence. I can't take it anymore," he responded. "I'm ready to do it."

"Do what?" I asked cautiously.

"Go all the way with God," Bill said exuberantly.

And he did. He committed himself to Christ fully that day. His whole life turned around. His marriage was better. His wife was thrilled. His kids even looked happier. But most importantly, Bill grew spiritually by leaps and bounds.

What made the difference? Total surrender. It's the first step to complete and total victory.

Postgame Highlights

1. *If I took score of my spiritual life, what would the score be?*

2. *At this rate, am I winning or losing?*

3. *What do I need to do now to ensure real victory in my life?*

Personal Interview

What is holding me back from total victory?

_____

_____

_____

_____

Final Wrap-up

There are no victories at bargain prices.

—General Dwight D. Eisenhower

CHAPTER

6

No More Excuses:

Overcoming Your Fears

We are all familiar with Murphy's Law: "Whatever can go wrong will go wrong!" When you get to the Book of the Judges, you come to one of those books where everything that could go wrong went wrong. Every problem we could imagine happened to the Israelites. And in every case, it was their own fault!

Once they had conquered the land and taken possession of God's inheritance, they decided to take it easy. Why keep fighting the enemy? We are winning, aren't we? After all, what could go wrong? Well, everything that could go wrong did go wrong! And the hope of the promise began to fade.

The Book of Judges revolves around six cycles of failure, repentance, and restoration. Six times the people are at ease. They fall into sin. God allows an enemy nation to come in and oppress them. They come under judgment. They cry out to God for a deliverer. They repent. God raises up a judge (the deliverer). The enemy is expelled. And a time of rest and prosperity follows. It worked like this:

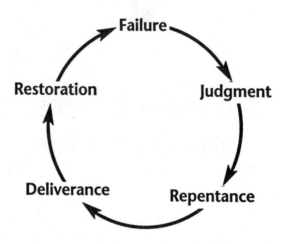

These cycles are true in our own lives. When we are doing what God wants us to do, everything goes well. That doesn't mean there aren't problems and difficulties in our lives. It means the hand of God's blessing is real in our lives. But when we get used to the blessing and start ignoring God, the enemy comes in, and everything goes wrong.

This is exactly what happened in the days of Gideon. Judges 6:1 says: "Again the Israelites did evil in the eyes of the LORD, and for seven years he gave them into the hands of the Midianites." The Midianites were desert bandits who came in off the Arabian desert to raid the farms of Israel. They would attack the people of the valleys, steal the food and cattle, destroy the villages, and chase the Israelites into the hills. For seven years in a row these bandits came back. Every time the Israelites had sown their crops and were ready to reap the harvest, the Midianites came and stole the crops. The results were devastating.

Imagine Ali Baba and 40,000 thieves! Thousands of Arab bandits coming in off the desert on their camels;

attacking the children of Israel; stealing their food, their women, and their animals; destroying their cities and then running back to the desert again. This went on for seven years! Until finally the children of Israel were broken before God. They repented of their sin and cried out to God for deliverance.

But this time God stepped back and said, "Wait a minute. We've been through this before! When are you going to learn your lesson? So you can get the point this time, I'm going to pick the most unlikely candidate I can find! A guy by the name of Gideon—*Super Chicken!* A guy so scared that he's afraid of his own shadow!"

An Unlikely Hero

There are two words that appear constantly throughout the story of Gideon: the word *if* and the word *fear. If* you really want me to do this—*if* this is what I'm supposed to do—*if–if–if.* Gideon never operates on faith and certainty. He's always raising the word *if* because he is afraid. Later, God turned him into something he was not. When we think of Gideon today, we think of a great hero. A great leader. There is even a great Christian organization named after him—the Gideons.

But Gideon started out in pretty bad shape. When the Lord first found him, he was hiding in a winepress. Judges 6:11

There are two words that appear constantly throughout the story of Gideon: the word if *and the word* fear.

says, "The angel of the Lord came...where...Gideon was threshing wheat in a winepress to keep it from the Midianites." A winepress was a deep hole lined with stones. You threw the grapes down in the winepress. Then someone would jump in and stomp the grapes.

Gideon was down inside the winepress, but he was not trying to make grape juice. He was in the winepress trying to thresh wheat! Normally, this was done on a threshing floor in an open field. Gideon was fearful that if he did it out in the open, the bandits would come in and steal the wheat from him. So he got down inside the winepress and tried to throw the grain up into the air through the opening. He must have looked ridiculous. He didn't even have enough room to operate. Imagine being cramped in a deep hole, trying to throw grain through the opening in the top. All the while, looking up to see if anyone was coming. And having the wheat fall back in your face. He had to have been covered from head to toe with the husks of grain!

About this time, the Bible says the angel of the Lord came along dressed like a shepherd and sat down under a tree next to the winepress. I'm sure he must have chuckled to himself. It would have been like looking at the open mouth of a well when, all of a sudden, up comes a pile of grain and down it goes again. Up and down—up and down—over and over again. Finally, the angel of the Lord decided he had better say something to this guy down there. So he said to him: "The LORD is with you, mighty warrior" (Judges 6:12).

Gideon probably thought, "Mighty warrior? Are you out of your mind? I'm scared to death! I'm down here in the winepress hiding for my life!"

"But sir," Gideon replied, "*if* the Lord is with us [the first of Gideon's many *ifs*], why has all this happened to us?... The LORD has abandoned us" (6:13). He was really saying, "Where is the power of God and His great miracles that our forefathers told us about? We haven't seen God do anything! Everything is going wrong!"

Instead of correcting him, criticizing him, or chastising him, the angel said, "Go in the strength you have and save Israel out of Midian's hand" (Judges 6:14).

"Go in my strength?" Gideon thought. "I don't have any strength! I'm Super Chicken down here. I'm hiding in a winepress. And you're out of your mind! You don't know who I am. I'm from the tribe of Manasseh, and we're the least of all the tribes! And I'm from the house of Joash, and we're the least of all the families in Manasseh. And I'm the least in my father's house. No way! You've got the wrong guy!"

God has a way of choosing unlikely candidates to do His work. He deliberately picked Gideon because he was such a coward. The old rabbis viewed Gideon not as a great warrior, but more like a bumbling oaf. Some years ago in the Hallmark series on television, this story was recreated with Peter Ustinov playing the part of Gideon. He portrayed a clumsy farmer who kept stumbling over his own shadow. Why had God chosen a coward to defeat Israel's enemies? He did it to teach them to trust His promises and not their own power.

Time Out

1. *What do God's choices tell us about His grace?*

2. *What are some of the weaknesses God had to overcome in your life?*

Overcoming Our Excuses

Most of us know the story of Gideon. He offered every possible excuse. But God would not let him get out of this obligation. Finally, Gideon said, "*If* now I have found favor in your eyes, give me a sign" (Judges 6:17). It was *if* number two. If this is for real, then do a miracle!

Gideon left to prepare a sacrifice. When he had finished and brought it out, the angel of the Lord asked him to put it on a rock. The Bible says the angel of the Lord took the staff in his hand and touched the rock. Instantly, fire came up out of the rock and consumed the entire offering. It scared Gideon to death! Gideon panicked and screamed, "I'm going to die! I'm going to die! I've seen God face-to-face. I'm going to die!"

Finally the angel looked at him and said, "Shut up—you're not going to die!" (That's my own paraphrase, but it captures the original thought.) The time for Gideon's excuses had come to an end. It was time for action! The angel commanded Gideon to tear down his father's Baal altar. Now, Baal was a Canaanite storm god. And Joash, an Israelite, had no business having it. And Gideon knew that but... "Tear it down? Are you crazy? He'll kill me!" Gideon thought.

The angel wouldn't take no for an answer. So Gideon tore down the Baal altar. But he got ten of his servants to help him, and he did it at night because "he was afraid of his family and the men of the town" (6:27). That simple phrase in the biblical text tells us how far the Israelites had strayed from God. They had totally forgotten the miraculous power of God. They were more afraid of public opinion than they were of God!

> *All too often, most of us sit back saying, "Somebody ought to do something." And God's reply usually is, "Why don't you do it?"*

By morning, the whole town was angry. They came to Joash's house, knocked on the door, and demanded, "Bring out Gideon! He tore down the Baal altar, and we're going to kill him!"

Joash couldn't believe it! "Gideon?" he thought. "He actually did something for once? He had enough nerve to take a stand? Who cares if it was against me? It's the greatest thing he's ever done!" His father was so impressed by the fact that Gideon was willing to take a stand that his dad came to his defense and told the men that if Baal were really a god, then Baal could plead his own case. "Let Baal defend himself," he suggested.

Then Gideon's father gave him a new name: *Jerrubabel.* In Hebrew it means "let Baal plead his own case." All too often, most of us sit back saying, "Somebody ought to do something. Somebody ought to stand up for God. Somebody ought to stand against secularism and paganism in our society. Somebody ought to tear down the Baal altar and raise the standard of God." And God's reply usually is, "Why don't you do it? When are you going to take a stand in your home? At your place of work? In your neighborhood and your community?"

God is still in the business of eliminating our excuses. An excuse is nothing more than a lie packaged to look like an explanation. As soon as Gideon, fearful as he was, took a stand, people were willing to follow him. What makes a person a leader? He has to be willing to lead. If you start leading, people will start following. But if you're not leading, no one is going to follow you. That is why everybody was in confusion, compromise, and defeat.

As soon as someone took a stand for what was right, people lined up to follow him. God took the most unlikely person imaginable, touched his life, and empowered him to win one of the most incredible victories in human history.

Halftime

1. What things do I fear most in life?

2. How can I learn to trust God with these fears?

No Turning Back

Before Gideon realized what he was doing, the Spirit of God "came upon" him, and he rallied an army against the Midianites. People came from all the surrounding towns and all the northern tribes: Manasseh, Naphtali, Asher, and Zebulun. They all showed up, saying, "We're here to follow you!"

Gideon thought, "I'm not used to being a leader. Now what am I going to do?" So he went back into his fear mode. He said, "I'll tell you what, God, *if* (here we go again) You really want me to do this, I need another indication to prove that this is Your will. Let's try a fleece." We often use the term *putting out the fleece.* But in reality, the fleece was *not* an act of faith. It was an act of fear!

The fleece was part of Gideon's hesitation. He wasn't ready to fully trust God yet. He was saying, "God, *if* You really want me to do it, here's what I'm going to do. I'll take this piece of wool and put it out on the threshing floor at night. When I get up in the morning, *if* the fleece is wet with dew and the ground around it is dry, I'll know for sure You want me to lead the children of Israel."

We often use the term "putting out the fleece." But in reality, the fleece was not *an act of faith. It was an act of fear!*

He got up the next morning and, sure enough, the fleece was wet and the ground was dry. It was so wet that he wrung out a whole bowl of water! But did he believe God and proceed? No! He implied, "How about two out of three? Let's flip again! How about this time the fleece is dry and the ground is wet?"

He got up the next morning and, sure enough, the fleece was dry and the ground was wet. God was not going to let him off the hook. There was no turning back now. The people came by the thousands to follow him.

They encamped at the spring of Harod which ironically in the Hebrew language means "the place of trembling." So here you have it. Cowardly Gideon with his army of farmers encamped at the "spring of trembling." You can just imagine who was doing the trembling!

This place still exists today. It's off the beaten path—just like it was then—but you can still find it. There is a natural spring at Harod, which overlooks part of the valley below. It was here that Gideon came with an army of 32,000 men. The problem is, there were 130,000 Midianites and Amalekites down in the valley. The Israelites were hideously outnumbered! In fact, the Scripture describes the invading horde as "grasshoppers"—like a plague of locusts swarming across the valley.

Gideon stood there thinking, "We're outnumbered! We don't stand a chance! We're doomed! What am I going to do?"

God spoke to Gideon and in essence said, "We've got a problem."

Gideon thought, "You're right! I don't have enough men!"

God said, "No, you've got too many men!"

Too many men? What do you mean, too many men? Gideon thought.

You've Got to Be Kidding!

God replied, "If I let 32,000 defeat 130,000 they're going to say, 'We did it ourselves!' I've been dealing with these people long enough to know how they operate. I want you to ask your men, 'How many are afraid?' Then tell the ones who admit it to go home."

Gideon probably thought, "Me! I'm afraid. And I want to go home!" But he went ahead and asked, "How many of you are afraid?" And 22,000 people raised their hands. And he had to tell them to leave. That left him with about 10,000 men—hardly enough to do the job.

I've never been in a battle, but I've been in a war zone during active combat in Africa. We would go to a town,

preach, and leave. And the next day, the town was rock-
eted with missiles. We talked to soldiers every day who
were being shot at in a terrible civil war. The soldiers
claimed there are three kinds of people in a battle. First,
they said anybody with any sense is afraid. And that covers
most people. That's why two-thirds of Gideon's army left.
Second, there are a bunch of guys who just want to fight.
They don't care if they get killed. They're going to stay
and fight. Most of the other third of Gideon's force was
probably like them.

The soldiers also told us about a third category of men in
battle. "They're the ones who are too afraid to admit they're
afraid," they explained. So when Gideon said, "If you're
afraid, raise your hand," they couldn't do it. They couldn't
even get their hands up. They were catatonic. They froze on
the battlefield–too afraid to admit they were afraid.

God said, "There are still too many men."

Too many men? Gideon thought.

"Take them down to the water, and I will sift them for you
there.... Separate those who lap the water with their tongues... from those who kneel down to drink" (Judges 7:4,5).

Now we have two groups of people: suckers and lappers. Everybody who just stuck his head down in the water
and sucked up a drink was put in one category. Then all
the lappers were put in another category. They were the
ones who scooped up the water in their hands and lapped
it with their tongues.

I've read almost every commentary ever written on the
Book of Judges. There is every kind of explanation for this
system of separation. Some say that the 300 guys who
lapped up the water were the wisest and best prepared.
They were the ones watching for the enemy. The rest
weren't paying attention. They just stuck their heads down
in the water to get a drink. Let me remind you, they were
up on the top of the mountain. The enemy is way down in
the valley. Nowhere near them! There was nothing to be
afraid of at that point.

The same old rabbis who viewed Gideon as a reluctant leader also viewed the 300 lappers as being afraid to take a drink. They thought, "There's a Midianite behind every rock. They're going to get us." But there wasn't anybody there! I believe God picked out the 300 biggest cowards He could find in Gideon's army and put him in charge of them!

When You're Too Afraid to Go On

By now, poor Gideon was catatonic himself. "How am I going to lead these guys to victory?" he wondered. "I've only got 300 men!"

That's when God intervened. "Get up, go down against the camp," He said.

You want me to go down to the camp of the Midianites? Gideon thought.

"If you are afraid to attack, go down to the camp with your servant Purah and listen to what they are saying," God suggested (Judges 7:10,11).

Next, the scripture says he took his servant Purah with him. Purah's name means "foliage." That's something to hide behind. Remember those old cowboy movies where they crept in behind the tumbleweed? That's the idea in this passage. Gideon is pushing the servant down the side of the mountain and saying, "I'm right behind you."

Something unusual happened when he got to the edge of the enemy camp. It was dark, and 130,000 men were asleep on the valley floor. Gideon came to the edge of the camp where two men were standing guard, talking to each other. And this is the conversation Gideon and his servant overheard.

"Man, I'm scared about this whole thing," one guard said to the other.

"Why are you so scared?" asked the other guard.

"I had the weirdest dream last night," he said. "I dreamed that a barley cake rolled down the side of this mountain and destroyed the whole army of the Midianites and the Amalekites!"

"What do you think it meant?" the other guard asked.

"I think it's Gideon! He's going to attack and kill us all!" he replied.

If there is anything that will encourage the heart of a coward, it is to find out that the enemy is more afraid of you than you are of him. Here was Gideon finding out they're afraid of him! With renewed confidence, he charged back up the hillside, aroused his troops and prepared to attack. It's old "barley cake" himself. "Hostess Twinkie" is going to take on the entire army!

I Know the Feeling

When I was a kid growing up in Detroit, my mother decided I needed to be in the Cub Scouts. So she signed me up and sent me off. Now in Detroit, the Cub Scouts didn't collect butterflies or rocks. They just fought all the time! Every time I would go to a den meeting, fights broke out. One day the den mother decided since we wouldn't stop fighting, we would have organized fighting–boxing matches. A boxing elimination–with a champion.

There was only one problem with this arrangement. One of the kids in our Cub Scout troop was an absolute monster! He was like a Tasmanian devil. And his name was Tim. Big Tim. He had a buzz haircut and a big, square jaw. Besides all that, he was ten years old!

When I was eight years old, Tim looked like he weighed 200 pounds. Like I said, he was a monster! "This is going to be a waste of time," we all thought. "Tim will beat all of us up!" They divided us into two groups. Fortunately for me, I was not in Tim's group. These poor little skinny guys would walk sheepishly into the ring with Tim. He would growl at them, stalk them into the corner, then pow! It was all over in one swing!

I was with a bunch of nerds who didn't know what they were doing. And I didn't know what I was doing either. We pushed each other around a little bit. Nobody even got hurt. But they kept announcing, "The winner—Hindson!" I won a couple of rounds by pure accident.

I was feeling pretty good until it occurred to me that if I won another round, I would win my division. And if I won my division, I would have to fight—TIM! I was in real trouble! So I thought I would take a dive as soon as the bell rang. But the other kid beat me to it!

The championship battle came around, and it was Little Edward against Big Tim. Scared as I was, a strange thought came to my mind. I had made an observation. Up to this point, nobody yet had ever hit Tim. They just backed up—and backed up—and *WHAM!*—he blasted them. So I began to think through my options. I could quit Cub Scouts and go home. Or I could just walk into the ring and take a dive. Or I could do something really crazy and stupid: I could wind up and hit him. See if anything happens. And if it doesn't, then run home and quit the Cub Scouts!

If there is anything that will encourage the heart of a coward, it is to find out that the enemy is more afraid of you than you are of him.

I was standing there scared to death. But I was not about to back up, because I knew he would get me. Which option would it be? The bell rang. I ran across the ring and hit Tim right in the mouth. It shocked him! Caught him by surprise! He wasn't expecting it! It couldn't possibly have hurt him, but it scared him. He started crying! And I went crazy—bam-bam-bam! I plummeted him! I went wild! Why? I found out the other guy was more afraid of me than I was of him. That's all it took!

That's what happened to Gideon. He couldn't believe it. The enemy was afraid of him! And he took courage in their fear. The Bible says, "Resist the devil, and he will flee from you" (James 4:7). All too often we let our fears overwhelm us, and we give up. But God says, "Don't give up. Get up! Take courage. Stand up. And trust Me!"

When God Has a Better Idea

Gideon came back to the Israelites raring to go. But God said, "I have a very unusual plan by which we're going to defeat the enemy. It's probably not what you had in mind. We're not going to go down and beat them up. We're going to *scare* them away!"

God has always had a great sense of humor. And it really shows in Gideon's case. He transformed a coward into a hero and scared the enemy away.

Gideon was so encouraged that he went back to the top of the hill ready to charge hell with a bucket of water. But God said, "Now wait a minute. I'm glad you finally got the courage to attack. But I've got a better idea!"

How easily we forget where we were when God found us. The fearful, hesitant coward is raring to go. And God had to hold him back. He had to remind Gideon that He was still the One in charge.

The Lord gave Gideon an incredible battle plan. He told him to take the 300 men and divide them into three groups. Put a pitcher with a torch in it in every man's hand. Then put a trumpet in their other hand. Then put 100 men on each side of the valley and 100 in the middle. Give the signal to break the pitchers, wave the torches, and blow on the trumpets. Then shout, "The sword of the Lord and Gideon!" That's it!

God used Gideon and his 300 lappers to scare the enemy away! When armies fought in ancient times, they rarely ever fought at night because they couldn't see anybody. Almost all of the battles in the ancient world were fought during the day. However, when they did fight at night, only a few soldiers carried a torch to try to light up the battlefield. Everybody carrying a torch could not carry a shield, which meant every torchbearer was undefended. So they would use only one torch for about every hundred men. That was usually enough light to see by.

They couldn't put a trumpet in every man's hand, either. Because if he has a trumpet in one hand, he would be missing a shield or a sword. Have you ever seen those Revolutionary War paintings? They had a little fife and drum corps. A few guys are playing on a piccolo and banging on a drum. Typically, there are about a dozen of them for every thousand soldiers. That was all!

Put the Enemy to Flight

A similar situation to Gideon's occurred in British history when the Scots were losing the Battle of Bannockburn. Word came from the battlefront that the Scots were retreating. In response, the old men and young boys at the Scottish camp picked up the flags and bagpipes and ran to the front. When they did, they made so much noise and kicked up so much dust that they put the enemy to flight!

The same thing happened when Gideon's enemies heard the smash of the pottery pitchers. It simulated the clash of arms and echoed down in the valley below. The noise woke up the Midianites and the Amalekites. All of a sudden they looked up and saw 300 torches and heard 300 trumpets all around them. They automatically assumed there must be 100,000 soldiers out there. They panicked, thinking the Israelites had hired allies to come against them. In the confusion of the noise and darkness, two different groups of people with two different dialects ran out of their tents. The Midianites and Amalekites slaughtered each other without even realizing it. Before the night was over, 120,000 Midianites and Amalekites had slain each other. And all Gideon and the 300 men had done was stand there and make some noise for God!

It doesn't take thousands of people to make a difference in the world in which we live. If a few people will get out and make some noise for God, and wave the light of the truth in the darkness, God will multiply and magnify their efforts. There is no telling what you and I could do for the cause of Christ if we really tried.

By the time Gideon put the enemy to flight, his whole army was so excited that the 300 men started to run down the hillside and chased the 10,000 who were left. Then other Israelites came from the surrounding hills and joined the fight. They chased after them, too. And before the day was over, the Israelites had wiped out nearly everybody. The few that survived ran into the desert and never came back.

The Promisor kept the promise alive! For the first time in a long time, the enemy respected the people of the promise and left them alone. They had taken a stand, scared the enemy away, and God had brought a tremendous victory through the leadership of an unlikely person with an unlikely army. "Super Chicken" and the "lappers" had prevailed.

God has always been in the business of doing the impossible. Sometimes it was the only way to keep the promise alive. And sometimes it was the only way to remind people that the Promisor was greater than the promise. The Bible reminds us: "God has not given us the spirit of fear: but of power, and of love, and of a sound mind" (2 Timothy 1:7, KJV). It's a lesson we all need to remember: God is more interested in our finding Him *in* life's struggles than protecting us *from* life's struggles.

Postgame Highlights

1. *What obstacles am I facing right now that really scare me?*

2. *How do I know God can get me through them?*

3. *What personal sacrifices will I have to make to get the job done?*

Personal Interview

What does God want me to trust Him with that I am afraid to give Him?

_____

_____

_____

_____

Final Wrap-up

You never conquer a mountain. You conquer yourself—your hopes—your fears.

–Jim Whittaker, first American
to climb Mt. Everest

CHAPTER
7

Keeping Your Promises:

Even When It Costs You!

Everybody wants to be loved. By nature, people crave acceptance, and they fear rejection. Nobody wants to be rejected. In fact, some people spend an entire lifetime in the pursuit of acceptance. They seek it in business, academics, athletics, and romance. Some people are so hungry for love and acceptance that they will pay any price to get it.

Others have been rejected so often that they have given up. They just settle for rejection as a normal part of life. Unfortunately, many times they reinforce their rejection through depressed behavior patterns such as drug or alcohol abuse.

The Book of Judges (Chapters 10-12) includes a strange story of acceptance and rejection. It, too, is set in a time when the promise seemed to be fading. It is a story about keeping your promises and not breaking your vows. It's the story of Jephthah the Gileadite—a most unusual hero.

The Bible says, "Jephthah the Gileadite was a mighty warrior. His father was Gilead; his mother was a prostitute" (Judges 11:1). Needless to say, this illegitimate son was not exactly the family favorite. In fact, Gilead's other sons expelled him from the family.

Hurt by their rejection, Jephthah fled to the Land of Tob, on the edge of the wilderness. There he gathered a band of rogues and rebels around him. And so he survived, but not without the pain of rejection in his heart.

After a while, the Ammonites from the Trans-jordan attacked the communities in the district of Gilead. And the family sent for Jephthah to come rescue them. What audacity! What hypocrisy! What desperation! His own relatives threw him out, and now they wanted him to come back and defend them.

Rejection may be undesirable, but it does have a way of toughening us to deal with the realities of life.

Rejection may be undesirable, but it does have a way of toughening us to deal with the realities of life. Just as the human body develops immunities to resist disease, likewise our personality develops skills to resist rejection. We can:

1. Avoid it.
2. Attack it.
3. Deny it.
4. Compensate for it.

Jephthah had become an expert at compensation. He had developed a barrier that would not allow anyone or anything to penetrate. He had become a "mighty warrior." He could take your head off and never flinch. But down inside, his heart longed for acceptance.

Nothing Like a Crisis to Pull Things Together

The Ammonite invasion was just what Jephthah needed—a chance to reconcile with his relatives, an opportunity to be restored to leadership and prominence.

"Come," they said, "be our commander, so we can fight the Ammonites" (Judges 11:6).

"Didn't you hate me and drive me from my father's house?" Jephthah responded. "Why do you come to me now, when you're in trouble?" (11:7).

So they promised to make him their captain and put him over all the cities of Gilead. Jephthah accepted their offer. Necessity is not only the "mother of invention," it is also often the "motive of acceptance." Nevertheless, the threat of a common enemy drew them all together.

Despite his background, Jephthah had a heart for God. The illegitimate son of a prostitute. A desert bandit. A social outcast. And yet, he was a man of great faith in God.

Perhaps the rejection he felt had driven Jephthah closer to God. He may have turned to the Lord as the only One who would accept him. People can feel rejected for a variety of reasons:

1. Personal rejection ("You don't want me.")
2. Social rejection ("Nobody wants me.")
3. Conditional love ("You only love me if...")
4. Deprivation of love ("You don't love me.")
5. Divorce ("You left me.")
6. Desertion ("You left us all.")
7. Dysfunction ("You don't understand me.")
8. Abuse ("You hurt me.")
9. Insecurity ("I don't like myself.")
10. Death ("You're not here for me.")

Jephthah may well have had to deal with several of these factors. Like many of the other judges of this period, he had to overcome great personal limitations and difficulties.

It is clear, however, that somewhere along the line, he had made peace with God over these issues.

In order to overcome rejection, we must come to grips with certain key factors in our lives. We must:

1. Accept God's love for us.
2. Stop blaming ourselves.
3. Stop blaming others.
4. Start living like a new person.

Most of us have to learn to deal with rejection sooner or later. You may have to overcome rejection from your own father, mother, family, or friends. While your life may be shaped by that rejection, it does not have to be limited by it. You can learn to overcome it. In fact, you can even become a better person because of it.

Time Out

1. Have you ever felt rejected? How? By whom?

2. How did you deal with it (or how are you dealing with it)?

Can't We Work This Out?

Jephthah tried to settle things out with peaceful negotiations, but it didn't work. He sent a message to the Ammonite king asking why he was invading their land. The king insisted that the land belonged to the Ammonites and that the Israelites took it from them in the conquest under Joshua.

"Wait a minute," Jephthah implied. "We never fought you over this land. We took it from other people. Besides, we've been here for over 300 years. Why haven't you raised this issue before?"

It didn't make sense, but then again, it didn't have to make sense. It's that same centuries-old argument over who owns this land–Jews or Arabs. Negotiations didn't work then much better than they do now.

Finally, Jephthah took his case to God. "Let the LORD, the Judge, decide the dispute this day between the Israelites and the Ammonites" (Judges 11:27).

This was an unusual appeal. It recognized then that God alone is sovereign over the land. Biblically speaking, He is the landlord and the people are His tenants. It also emphasizes that God can give the land to whomever He chooses. So on this basis, Jephthah appealed to God to settle the issue. After all, He was and still is the ultimate Judge.

Unfortunately, the Ammonite king rejected Jephthah's appeal, and he continued to advance toward the Israelites. The Jews and "Jordanians" were preparing to face off.

Promises, Promises

Then it happened, just like it did to Gideon: "The Spirit of the LORD came upon Jephthah" (11:29). He rallied a great army and crossed Gilead and Manasseh to meet the enemy at Mizpah. En route to the battle, he made a solemn vow to God: "If you give the Ammonites into my hands, whatever comes out of the door of my house to meet me when I return in triumph from the Ammonites will be

A vow was a solemn promise to God. It represented not only a man's word, but his character.

the LORD's, and [some translations have "or"] I will sacrifice it as a burnt offering" (11:30,31).

A vow was a solemn promise to God. The Hebrew term *nadar* conveys the idea of a consecration to God, meaning a serious commitment or pledge. It represented not only a man's word, but his character. Such vows were not to be made or taken lightly. Psalm 50:14 (KJV) says, "Offer to God a sacrifice of thanksgiving, and pay your vows to the Most High."

In the New Testament, Jesus reminds us to speak the truth when we take an oath or make a vow. "Let your 'Yes' be 'Yes' and your 'No,' 'No,'" He teaches (Matthew 5:37). The keeping of one's word was viewed as a serious matter. It meant the keeping of a covenant and, ultimately, the honor of one's character.

The Promise Keepers phenomenon now sweeping our country is right in line with this biblical practice. It encourages men to make and keep seven basic promises:

1. Honor Jesus Christ through worship, prayer, and obedience to God's Word through the power of the Holy Spirit.
2. Pursue vital relationships with a few other men, understanding that we need brothers to help us keep our promises.
3. Practice spiritual, moral, ethical, and sexual purity.
4. Build strong marriages and families through love, protection, and biblical values.
5. Support the mission of the church by honoring and praying for your pastor and by actively giving time and resources.
6. Reach beyond any racial and denominational barriers to demonstrate the power of biblical unity.
7. Influence the world, being obedient to the Great Commandment (Mark 12:30,31) and the Great Commission (Matthew 28:19,20).

Jephthah's vow was certainly made in all sincerity. And he did, in fact, win a great triumph over the Ammonites.

He returned home in triumph as Israel's great hero, lauded by his neighbors and welcomed by the excited throng.

But when Jephthah reached his house, to his utter dismay, his own daughter ran out to meet him dancing for joy and playing a tambourine (Judges 11:34). It wasn't a sheep or a goat. It was his only child! And he had promised to sacrifice her to God as a burnt offering.

Now what would he do?

Many new believers make the mistake of overcommitting themselves. They are so excited about their new life in Christ that they want to experience everything they can. So they volunteer for every job in the church. The problem is, they often do so at the expense of their families.

Alan was so committed to his church that he spent more time there than he did at home. At first, Diane was impressed by Alan's zeal. But eventually she began to feel neglected.

"Can't you help me paint the kitchen?" she asked one Saturday.

"No, I've got to help paint the fellowship hall at church," he replied.

"What about Danny's baseball game this afternoon?"

"You know I go on visitation every Saturday afternoon!" he shot back. "I've got to help Jack pick up those kids we're trying to reach."

"What about our kids?" Diane pleaded as he rushed out the door.

It all began so innocently. Alan was honestly trying to do the right things at church. But he became so overcommitted that he began doing the wrong things at home. Eventually, it cost him his family.

Diane gave up all hope that he would change. She took the kids and went to live with her mother. Alan was shocked and begged her to come back. But it was too late. Nothing he said could persuade her to change her mind. Within a year they were divorced. Diane was mad at God and dropped out of church altogether. And Alan became so confused and bitter that he dropped out as well.

Halftime

1. *Have you ever made a promise that you later wished you had not made?*

2. *Have you ever made a vow that really cost you sacrificially?*

3. *Would God ask us to keep a promise that violated His word?*

Keeping Your Word

Jephthah's vow was made in good faith. The question is, What did it involve? One view is that he promised to sacrifice *whatever* came out of his house as a burnt offering to God. In those days, animals were often kept in the house. Anything could have come out of his house: a sheep, a goat, or a cow (which happen to be appropriate sacrifices). But a dog or cat or mouse could have come running out of his house as well. And those animals would not have been an appropriate sacrifice to God.

That is why some translators prefer to translate the passage: "Whatever comes out of my house...will be the Lord's *or* I will sacrifice it as a burnt offering." The original Hebrew allows for either translation. That way if what comes out of the house is not appropriate for sacrifice, it can be dedicated to God's service.

For example, in biblical times, animals not suitable for sacrifice could be given to the priest and sold. The proceeds would then go to the Temple. Leviticus 27 gives various amounts to be paid for the redemption of persons who had been vowed to the Lord or animals which had been dedicated to the Tabernacle.

The issue at stake over Jephthah's vow is whether or not he actually slew his own daughter and offered her as a burnt sacrifice to God. Commentaries on this passage are equally divided over whether he did or did not actually kill her.

Notice what the text itself says about what happened:

1. He was brokenhearted over the vow (verse 35).
2. His daughter accepted it: "Do to me just as you promised" (verse 36).
3. She asked for a two-month delay to weep because "she would never marry" (verses 37, 38).
4. He later fulfilled the vow: "He did to her as he had vowed" (verse 39).

The Bible does not actually say that he sacrificed her. It says only that he kept his promise to the Lord. Now it is often suggested that Jephthah was a rogue, the son of a harlot, and a man of war. Therefore, it is implied that he could have killed her.

However, consider the reasons why he would *not* have killed her:

1. Child sacrifice was forbidden by the Law of Moses (Leviticus 20:2-5; Deuteronomy 18:10).
2. Child killers are universally condemned in Scripture: king of Moab (2 Kings 3:26,27), Ahaz (2 Chronicles 28:3), Manasseh (2 Kings 21:6), and Herod (Matthew 2:16).
3. Jephthah had just defeated the Ammonites, who were notorious for child-sacrifice to the gods Molech and Chemosh.
4. God would not let Abraham sacrifice Isaac to Him (Genesis 22:12).
5. Jephthah is described as being filled with the Holy Spirit (Judges 11:29).
6. The daughter eagerly accepted the consequences of the vow—perpetual virginity (not death).

7. The Israelites commemorated this vow every year as an annual practice (Judges 11:40). It is highly unlikely they would have celebrated a wrong or sinful decision.

Baby Dedication Is Serious Business

Dedicating a child to the Lord's service was a common Old Testament practice. Samuel's mother "loaned" him to the LORD. She presented him to Eli, the priest at the Tabernacle. And she said: "So now I give him to the LORD. For his whole life he will be given over to the Lord" (1 Samuel 1:28). Samuel was given to God's service shortly after his mother weaned him at age three or four.

We also read about "young virgins" dancing at the annual festival of the Lord at the Tabernacle in Shiloh (Judges 21:19-22). Those mentioned in this passage were taken by the Benjamites to be their wives. Thus, the precedent of dedicating a daughter to the Lord's service in a life of perpetual virginity is well established in Bible history.

I believe that Jephthah fulfilled his vow by dedicating his daughter to God's service. This would mean she could never marry or bear him any grandchildren. Though victorious in battle, he would have no offspring to perpetuate his family line. In ancient times, this was considered a grave tragedy.

His daughter's perpetual virginity was certainly something for her to weep about for two months with her friends (Judges 11:38). And her dedication to God as a lifelong virgin was certainly worth commemorating in an annual festival. Furthermore, that she wasn't actually killed helps explain why she didn't run away.

No other view of this passage makes any real sense when compared to biblical evidence. Even the text itself does *not* say that he actually killed her or sacrificed her as a burnt offering. It says only that he fulfilled the vow (verse 39). If the vow allowed for either sacrifice or dedication, then he clearly would have chosen the latter option.

This would mean that the original vow should be translated: "Whatever comes out of the door of my house...will be the Lord's *or* I will sacrifice it as a burnt offering" (11:31). There is no way he could have left this vow wide open to include sacrificing his wife, daughter, dog, or cat. Such an act would have been totally inappropriate.

Whatever view one takes on *how* Jephthah fulfilled the vow, the fact remains *that* he fulfilled it. It cost him dearly either way. He was devastated. His heart was broken because the keeping of his vow meant that he would have no heirs. His family line would be cut off. Thus, his great victory was bittersweet at best.

Dedicating Ourselves to God

Every time a couple comes to dedicate their children to God, they are really dedicating themselves to God. The ultimate significance of their act of dedication is their promise to raise their children by their Christlike example. Their dedication of themselves is what will really make a difference in their children's lives.

When a baby is born into a godly home, he or she has a wonderful opportunity to be raised in a committed Christian atmosphere. But that atmosphere alone won't change the child's life. Neither will christening services nor dedication ceremonies. Only the Spirit of God can transform the human heart.

That's why God challenges us to raise our children by His principles. The Bible is filled with parental admonitions:

> "These commandments that I give you today
> are to be upon your hearts. Impress them on
> your children" (Deuteronomy 6:6,7).

Train a child in the way he should go, and when he is old he will not turn from it" (Proverbs 22:6).

My son, give me your heart and let your eyes keep to my ways" (Proverbs 23:26).

Children, obey your parents in the Lord, for this is right.... Fathers, do not exasperate your children; instead, bring them up in the training and instruction of the Lord" (Ephesians 6:1,4).

The emphasis on *accountability* in Scripture rests solely with the parents. We are accountable to God for how we raise our children. The Bible clearly emphasizes the importance of parental:

1. Image: What we are.
2. Influence: What we do.
3. Instruction: What we say.

If our example contradicts our instruction, we send a confusing message to our children. Whether we realize it or not, they are watching us as well as listening to us. And we need to be *showing* them as well as *telling* them what to do. Parents model behavior as much as they teach it.

Ask yourself, Does my life back up my instruction? Am I saying, "Do as I do," or am I really saying, "Do as I say"? Consistency is the key to parental example. It is the most effective way to reinforce your instruction and solidify your dedication. When you are determined to be the godly example your children need, God will bless them through your influence.

Fathers are especially important in a child's development. Your children need to know their dad will be there for them when they need him. They need to be able to look up to you for strength and security. And they need to know they can count on you at every stage of their development.

Your children ought to be able to look at you and say, "If anybody knows God, my dad does! I can tell by the way he lives, by the way he talks, and by the things he does."

If our children cannot look at us and tell what is really important to us, we are failing to communicate our values. The things we spend our time and money on are the most important things in our lives. And the people we spend our time with are the most important people in our lives.

If our children cannot look at us and tell what is really important to us, we are failing to communicate our values.

If your children evaluated your life, what would they most likely say about your love for them, their mother, and God? The answers to those questions tell them who you really are. They also speak volumes about what is really important to you.

Recently, Dr. James Dobson broadcast a program on "Focus on the Family" that emphasized keeping your marriage vows. In that broadcast a guest shared that he began writing notes to his wife that underscored the various elements of his wedding vows. Depending on their circumstances, he would jot her a note and add: "in sickness and in health," or "till death do us part," or "forsaking all others," or "for richer, for poorer." And then he would sign his name.

Those little notes, with phrases from his wedding vows, were his way of saying, "Honey, you can count on me!" It's a great idea—one we could all benefit from—because it personalizes and puts into practice our vows and commitments. It reminds us that we must live out what we have said we will do.

Making promises is one thing. Keeping them is another. Going from a promise maker to a keeper of promises begins in your own heart. It begins by giving yourself totally to God and letting Him become the object of your love and devotion. Only when you are fully committed to Him can you become fully committed to your wife and children. Only then can you really keep your promises.

Postgame Highlights

1. *Do you have a difficult time keeping your promises?*

2. *What usually goes wrong?*

3. *What should you do differently in the future?*

Personal Interview

In what areas do you need to be a better example to your children?

_____

_____

_____

Final Wrap-up

Our calling is to exhibit God and His character, by His grace, in this generation.

—Francis Shaeffer

Language Highlights

1. Do you have problems telling right to left?

2.

3.

Personal Interview

What's Up?

CHAPTER

8

Facing Your Weaknesses:
Making Them Your Strengths

Wine, women, and food," Bill said, shaking his head. "That's what most men struggle with." He paused for a few seconds and added, "And maybe sports, too!"

It was quite an admission from a guy who wasn't used to self-analysis. In fact, it took everything he had to say that much. Of course, he left off a whole list of other problem areas: pride, arrogance, materialism, anger, jealousy, envy, greed, and self-indulgence. But it was a start.

Bill's wife had already made a similar observation. "If he can't eat it, drink it, kick it, or sleep with it, he's not interested in it," she said.

After discussing these issues for a while, I asked Bill, "What are you going to do about these temptations?"

He pulled back in his seat as though I had hit a sensitive nerve. He scowled, grimaced, and said, "Hey, everybody's got weaknesses! Why should I be any different?"

Now, that raises an important question: What difference does it make if we have a few weaknesses? We all fall short, don't we?

The battle with temptation is not unique to you. It is a universal problem. Everyone faces temptation in one form or another. For some, the struggle is *internal:* guilt, fear, worry, depression. For others, the struggle is *external:* sex, money, fame, and fortune.

> *One reason we don't deal with temptation more effectively is our refusal to admit we have a problem with it.*

The Bible reminds us: "No temptation has seized you except what is common to man" (1 Corinthians 10:13). You're not the only one struggling with temptation. We all face it! For some, it is a daily struggle. For others, it's an occasional battle. But for all of us, the battle is a reality of life.

One reason we don't deal with temptation more effectively is our refusal to admit we have a problem with it. The Scripture says, "But each one is tempted when, by his own evil desire, he is dragged away and enticed" (James 1:14). This puts the blame entirely on me. It's my fault when I am tempted because I am the *source* of the temptation.

Bill didn't like where this discussion was going. So he blurted out, "Eat, drink, and be merry, for tomorrow we die! That's my philosophy," he insisted.

"Yes," I agreed, "but remember, all too often we *don't* die. We just live to suffer the consequences of eat, drink, and be merry!"

We live in a nation filled with alcoholism, gluttony, and sexual indulgence. Excessive self-gratification has men on the fast track to self-destruction. And the real tragedy is that many men refuse to admit it. They won't slow down long enough to take a good look at what they are doing to themselves.

A Biblical Parallel

One of the most memorable stories in the Bible is that of Samson. He was born into a poor Jewish family in the remote outskirts of the Valley of Sorek. It was a rural area near Beth Shemesh that snuggled up to the border of the Philistines during the days of the judges.

Times were tough for the Israelites. They had struggled for more than 200 years to keep their foothold in the Promised Land. Now they had a new problem: Philistines. These European "sea people" sailed across the Mediterranean and landed on the coast of Israel in about 1200 B.C.

In a short time, the Philistines captured all the good farmland along the coast. The Israelites retreated to the hill country and tried to survive as best they could. One of the tribes hardest hit was the tribe of Dan, which directly bordered on the Philistine land. They were also the weakest of the 12 tribes of Israel.

Things were so bad that the Danites gave up their tribal inheritance and fled north (cf. Judges 18), which left only a few families dwelling in "refugee camps" along the edge of the Valley of Sorek. It was into one of these families that Samson was born. Ironic as are many other accounts in Judges, the strongest man who ever lived came from the weakest tribe Israel ever had.

Samson's name (Hebrew, *shimshon*) means "sunny" or "of the sun." It may reflect the name of nearby Beth Shemesh ("house of the sun"). In any case, he was a bright young man with a brilliant future. Despite his family's poverty and his tribe's weakness, Samson was endowed by the Spirit of God with incredible, superhuman strength.

Even as a boy growing up in the refugee camp, Samson showed unusual feats of strength. The Bible says, "The Spirit of the LORD began to move him at times in the camp of Dan" (Judges 13:25, KJV). But this unusual Hebrew hunk remained relatively unknown until he was a young man.

By the time he was about 20 years old, Samson commonly wandered freely across the border into Philistine territory. On one of these jaunts, he fell in love at first sight with a Philistine girl in Timnah. His major weakness now became evident: He had an eye for the ladies.

A Nice Jewish Boy Like You?

The wanderer had a wandering eye. He was especially attracted to beautiful Philistine women. He fell so hard for the young girl from Timnah that he virtually lost his mind.

Whenever we put pleasure ahead of principle, we are headed for trouble.

"I have seen a Philistine woman in Timnah," he told his Jewish parents. "Now get her for me as my wife" (Judges 14:2).

A Philistine! They were horrified. Uncircumcised Gentiles! Pagans! "Isn't there an acceptable woman...among all our people?" they pleaded. "Must you go to the uncircumcised Philistines to get a wife?" (verse 3).

But Samson's mind was made up. His heart was smitten. His hormones were aroused. His genes were calling. And he wasn't going to take no for an answer.

"Get her for me. She's the right one for me," he insisted.

Whenever we put pleasure ahead of principle, we are headed for trouble. It is only a matter of time before disaster strikes.

Samson's selfishness, lust, and pride would eventually become his downfall. Before he was born, the angel of the Lord appeared to his mother and announced that he would be a Nazirite ("separated one"). The Nazirite vow included three strict prohibitions:

1. Do not touch or eat anything "unclean."
2. Do not drink wine or other fermented drink.
3. Do not cut your hair.

These were external signs of his internal commitment to God. This was no ordinary child. He was a "holy child," uniquely dedicated to God. And he was uniquely endowed with great human strength by the Holy Spirit. His strength came from God, not from the length of his hair. His hair was only an outward symbol of God's calling on his life.

Samson's parents reluctantly agreed to go with him to Timnah to meet the girl's parents. While they went on ahead, Samson lingered at the vineyards outside the town. Before we move on, let's ask a question: What grows in vineyards? Grapes. What is Samson supposed to resist? Wine. So what is going on here? He is lingering in a place of temptation and vulnerability.

Samson was probably thinking, "Grapes! Look at all those grapes! I wonder what they taste like? One little grape can't hurt anything."

Now keep in mind that it wasn't the grapes that were the problem, but Samson's curiosity. It was his curiosity that led him to the place of temptation. So, God sent an interruption to get his attention.

Just then, a lion leaped out of the vineyard and attacked him. The Spirit of the Lord came upon him, and he "tore the lion apart with his bare hands" (14:6). It was an incredible feat of strength! But the Bible says, "He told neither his father nor his mother what he had done." Why? He didn't want to admit his vulnerability.

Time Out

1. *Why is it so difficult for men to admit their weaknesses?*

2. *What are your weaknesses? Where are you vulnerable to temptation?*

The Slippery Slide

Samson tossed the lion's carcass aside and went into town. It must have been a very difficult day for his Jewish parents. They felt forced into making the wedding arrangements with this Gentile family. If you have ever attended a wedding between a believer and a nonbeliever, you can imagine the tension and heartache they felt. It was the beginning step in the wrong direction.

When Samson returned to marry the Philistine girl, he came upon the vineyards again. Out of curiosity, he turned aside to look at the lion's carcass. To his surprise, a swarm of bees had settled into the dehydrated carcass and filled it with honey.

Without hesitating, Samson scooped out the honey and ate it (14:8,9). He even gave some to his parents. But he didn't dare tell them where it came from. Why not? Anything that was dead was considered "unclean" by the Mosaic law. Samson had just violated the first stipulation of the Nazirite vow.

This incident gives us a glimpse into the soul and character of the man. Samson let his feelings control him. Though he was a man of strength, he could not control his own appetites. He lusted after the girl. He flirted with temptation. He disregarded his spiritual heritage. He violated his religious vows. And he broke his promises.

It wasn't long until one violation led to another. It was customary for Philistine bridegrooms to throw a "drinking feast" (Hebrew, *mishteh*) for the groomsmen. It was like a bachelor's party and beer blast the night before the wedding. Interestingly, modern archaeologists have uncovered hundreds of Philistine wine bottles, beer jugs, and whiskey flasks. They were notorious drinkers. And Samson became one of the boys that night.

If Samson threw the party (cf. 14:10), we can safely assume he drank at the party. Thus, he violated the second stipulation of the Nazirite vow. The holy man got drunk.

The unique Nazirite was a regular "party animal." Like many believers, he stepped over a line he said he would never cross.

Think of the times in your own life when you said, "I would never do that." And you went right ahead and did it! Once we break our promises and violate our vows, we are filled with guilt. And guilty people become arrogant, negative, critical, and even hostile. One wrong step leads to a slippery downfall.

One Good Turn Deserves Another

Samson was mad at himself, so he took out his frustration on the Philistines. He gave them a riddle to expose their ignorance that had to do with the honey in the lion's carcass: "Out of the eater, something to eat; out of the strong, something sweet" (Judges 14:14).

The Philistines had no idea what he was talking about. Who had ever found honey in a lion? They were totally stumped. So they went to his wife during the seven-day wedding reception and threatened her.

"Coax your husband into explaining the riddle for us, or we will burn you and your father's household to death" (14:15), they threatened.

Instead of confiding in her new husband, Samson's wife pressured him to tell her the riddle. She badgered him and nagged him the entire seven days of the wedding reception. But he wouldn't budge.

"You hate me!" she whined. "You don't really love me. You've given my people a riddle, but you haven't told me the answer" (verse 16).

Then Samson said something very revealing to his new bride: "I haven't even explained it to my father or mother...so why should I explain it to you?"

Brilliant! He put his parents above his wife. Great move, Samson. Now you're really in trouble!

She cried and hollered all the more. Refusing his every advance, she nagged him until he couldn't stand it anymore. Finally, he broke down and told her on the last day of the reception. Then she ran and told the Philistines, and they "guessed" the riddle at the last possible moment. "What is sweeter than honey? What is stronger than a lion?" they suggested (verse 18).

Samson immediately knew he had been betrayed. "If you had not plowed with my heifer, you would not have solved my riddle," he responded in disgust.

He had been married only a week, and he was already calling his wife an old cow! In anger, he stormed out of the reception before the wedding ceremony was officially consummated. Following the custom of the day, the girl was married off to the best man ("friend of the bridegroom") in Samson's absence.

Two Wrongs Don't Make a Right

When Samson finally returned to Timnah, he was shocked to find his "wife" married to someone else.

Samson blew up! He couldn't believe it. He stormed out more angry than ever. He gathered 300 foxes (or jackals), tied their tails together, lit them on fire, and let them loose in the wheat fields. The frightened animals ran everywhere, lighting the fields ablaze. The fire spread out of control and burned up the Philistine vineyards and the olive groves as well.

Two wrongs don't make a right. The Philistines were so angered by this devastating loss that they blamed it on the girl and her father and burned them to death in their house. The very fate she sought to avoid by revealing the riddle happened to her anyway. She failed to confide in her own husband, and it cost her her life.

In the meantime, the Philistines chased after Samson. His own countrymen from the tribe of Judah handed him over to the Philistines. But when they came to get him,

"The Spirit of the LORD came upon him in power" (Judges 15:14). The "Hebrew Hulk" broke loose, grabbed the jawbone of a donkey, and slew a thousand Philistines.

When the day ended, dead bodies were everywhere. The rest had fled for their lives. And Samson stood victorious, holding the jawbone. There was only one problem–it was "unclean!"

Halftime

1. *Have you ever compromised your convictions to satisfy your desires?*

2. *What goes wrong when we break our promises to God?*

Will We Ever Learn?

Samson's first encounter with the Philistines ends with the statement that he judged Israel for 20 years (15:20). The same thing is repeated after his infamous encounter with Delilah (16:31). It is generally assumed, therefore, that 20 years passed between his marriage to the girl at Timnah and his affair with Delilah.

The ultimate tragedy in Samson's life was that he never learned his lesson the first time. The whole drama was repeated 20 years later. He had annihilated enough Philistines to make them all afraid of him. He wandered about unrestrained, even taking forays into various Philistine cities such as Gaza, whose gates he ripped off (16:1-3).

During those 20 years the Philistines left the Israelites alone for fear of Samson. He was like a one-man army. And the Philistines kept their distance.

But the old weaknesses were still there: a lustful heart, a wandering eye, and selfish desires. Eventually, those weaknesses cost him everything. At about age 40, he fell in love with a notorious Philistine beauty named Delilah. She was not a novice, like the first girl. Delilah was a mature, sensuous, selfish woman. She knew how to use her feminine wiles to get exactly what she wanted from men.

Their romantic affair drew national attention. Before long, the Philistine leaders paid her a visit. They each promised to give her 1100 shekels of silver if she could deliver Samson to them. Historians tell us that the Philistines were ruled by five "lords" (Hebrew, *Tseren*). That would mean they were offering her 5500 pieces of silver—a huge fortune for any woman.

A Deadly Lover's Game

I have always pictured Delilah like a Joan Collins character: mature, beautiful, sexy, crafty, selfish, and downright nasty. One has only to read the biblical text to get the same idea. She didn't even hesitate to agree to their deal to deliver Samson to them. She quickly began the deadly lover's game that would cost Samson his life.

"Tell me the secret of your great strength," she suggested, "and how you can be tied up and subdued" (16:6).

This simple request soon became part of a daily game between them. She would admire his great strength and then ask, "How could little ol' me tie up big Samson?"

Surprisingly enough, he went along with the whole thing. "If anyone ties me with seven fresh thongs that have not been dried, I'll become as weak as any other man," he told her (16:7).

Thongs were used in warfare, and she didn't have any. So the Philistines brought her the thongs. She tied him up while he was asleep. Then she shouted, "Samson, the Philistines are upon you!" Samson jumped up and snapped the thongs effortlessly.

"You have made a fool of me," Delilah protested. "You lied to me. Come now, tell me how you can be tied" (16:10).

And so the game continued, probably over a period of several days or even weeks. Every time he came to see her for romantic purposes, she would ask him how she could tie him up.

"If anyone ties me securely with new ropes that have never been used, I'll become as weak as any other man," he told her the next time (16:11).

> *Once we start down the slippery slope of sin, it is difficult to recover.*

Ropes? She had ropes. She tied him up herself.

"Samson, the Philistines are upon you!" she shouted.

Again, he awoke and snapped the ropes. And again, she protested. Perhaps she pouted. Perhaps he teased her. But she finally insisted, "Until now, you have been making a fool of me and lying to me. Tell me how you can be tied" (16:13).

Her requests implied an element of trust. "Don't you trust me enough to tell me your secret?" How could he make love to her, take advantage of her, and not tell her his great secret?

Compromise always leads to capitulation. Once we start down the slippery slope of sin, it is difficult to recover.

Lowering Your Guard

Samson began to weaken. "If you weave the seven braids of my head into the fabric on the loom and tighten it with the pin, I'll become as weak as any other man" (16:13).

It still wasn't the truth, but it was dangerously close. I'm convinced she knew it was, too. She was an experienced woman. She could probably tell he had been lying to her all along. That's why she kept probing to find the secret.

In ancient Near Eastern homes, there was generally a weaving loom attached to a cross beam in the ceiling.

Every woman of status had one. It was usually her pride and joy. Whether Delilah ever used hers much may be debatable. But this time she went right to work braiding his hair and weaving it into the pattern on the loom.

"That hair," she may have thought. "What's with all this hair, anyway? Finally, it's done!"

"Samson," she shouted again, "the Philistines are upon you!"

This time he awoke, jerked his head, and "pulled up the pin and the loom, with the fabric" (16:14).

"That's it!" she may have shouted. "You've wrecked my sewing machine!"

She apparently threw a fit and told him off. Then he tried to console her and tell her that he loved her. But she was too angry to respond. She evidently pushed him away.

"How can you say, 'I love you,' when you won't confide in me?" she demanded. "This is the third time you have made a fool of me and haven't told me the secret of your great strength" (16:15).

Now she had him on the defensive. She kept pursuing him day after day. The Bible actually says she nagged him to death (16:16). He couldn't take it anymore. He finally broke and told her everything.

A Haircut in the Devil's Barbershop

"No razor has ever been used on my head," he explained, "because I have been a Nazirite set apart to God since birth. If my head were shaved, my strength would leave me, and I would become as weak as any other man" (16:17).

This time she had him, and she knew it! She realized he was finally telling her the truth. The tone of his voice and the look on his face gave it away. The King James Version says he told her "all his heart." A woman can tell when she's being lied to, and she can tell when a man is being really honest with her. All the rest had been a game. But this was the truth.

Delilah immediately sent for the Philistine rulers and instructed them to bring the silver with them.

"Come back once more," she urged them. "He has told me everything" (16:18).

While Samson was asleep on her lap, a man crept into the room and shaved off his hair. Then she began pounding on his chest, shouting, "Samson, the Philistines are upon you!"

However, she was the only Philistine afflicting him. She hated him! Perhaps she hated all men. She was tired of being used, and it was her turn. She was now rich and free. Many men have lost their dignity over a woman, but Samson lost far more.

"I'll go out as before," Samson thought, "and shake myself free." But he did not realize that God had departed from him (16:20).

There he stood. Totally bald. His beautiful hair was gone. He rushed at the Philistines in naked stupidity.

The Bible reminds us that with every temptation, God provides a "way of escape."

This time, the Philistines captured him and gouged out his eyes. Then they bound him in bronze shackles and led him off to the prison house in Gaza. He was taken back to the very city whose gates he had stolen. But this time he was bald, blind, and bound. The "Hebrew Hulk" had been subdued.

Dealing with Temptation

Samson failed to deal with temptation and paid a terrible price for it. The Bible reminds us that with every temptation, God provides a "way of escape" (1 Corinthians 10:13, KJV). But we have to be willing to take it. The following are some practical steps for dealing with temptation:

1. *Take a good look at yourself.* Honest self-analysis is the first step toward progress. If your life is going to be renewed, you must be honest with God and with yourself.

2. *Admit you have a problem.* Rationalizing your sins will never cure them. Confess your faults to the Father. Stop denying the obvious. Face up to your weaknesses. And determine to do something about them.

3. *Believe that God can make a difference in your life.* Doubting believers are never victorious believers. God has promised to deliver those who will trust in Him. You need more faith, not more self-effort.

4. *Make a total commitment.* There are no halfhearted victories in the battle with temptation. Total surrender to the will of God is the key to victory. You must come to the point where you let God take total control of your life.

5. *Renewal is a full-time job.* Live out your new commitment daily. Read the Word. Pray to the Father. Be filled with the Spirit. Live like a believer. Let God make the difference in your life.

6. *Take the "way of escape"!* Stay away from the source of your temptation. Don't hang out in vulnerable places with questionable people. When God's Spirit convicts your heart, listen–then leave!

Each one of us has a "window of time" to take the "way of escape." Samson waited too long and paid dearly. The consequences of his sin were humiliation and defeat. The Philistines took him to Gaza and shackled him to a grinding mill. The man who had been betrayed by a woman was sentenced to do a woman's work.

When You're Out of Options

In the meantime, the Bible notes that Samson's hair began to grow again (Judges 16:22). But his strength did not return because his strength was not in the length of his hair. His strength came from the Spirit of God. Remember, the hair was only an outward symbol of his inner dedication. Since he had earlier violated the other stipulations of the Nazirite vow, his long hair was the only one remaining. When it was cut, the power of the vow was completely broken.

If Samson's strength had returned when his hair began to grow, the Philistines would have buzzed his head regularly. But they didn't have to. Instead, they tried to make sport of him by putting him on display during the festival of Dagon, the Philistine grain god. So they tied him to the temple pillars while 3000 men and women laughed and jeered in his face.

It was then that Samson truly repented for the first and last time. "O God," he prayed, "strengthen me just once more. . . . Let me die with the Philistines!"

There was little else a blind warrior could do. He had no following. No soldiers. No army. Remember, he had always been a one-man army. But now he could no longer see the enemy. Killing thousands of Philistines in his own death was all he could do.

In fact, it was the one unselfish thing he ever did do. His death was an act of self-sacrifice on behalf of those he had failed.

Reaching for the pillars of the Greek-style temple, Samson slid them off their stone bases. The weight of the stone roof shifted, and the whole structure fell like a deck of cards. An earthquake could not have been more devastating. The wreckage was strewn everywhere with thousands of twisted, screaming bodies crushed beneath the building's stones.

Thousands of Philistines were dead, and so was Samson. His family, like the other mourners, dug his body out of the rubble and took it home for burial. It was a dark day in Israel's history. Their greatest warrior was dead. And their hopes and dreams died with him.

The promise never seemed more bleak than it did in those days. Moral compromise led to political collapse and civil catastrophe. By the end of the Book of Judges, the writer could only say, "In those days Israel had no king; everyone did as he saw fit" (21:25).

But God had not forgotten His promises. He was still in the business of turning weaknesses into strengths. He could still bring sunshine out of darkness.

Postgame Highlights

1. *What nagging habits still remain as trouble spots in your Christian life?*

2. *Are you really facing them honestly, or are you still living in denial?*

Personal Interview

What changes need to occur in your life in order for you to avoid personal disaster?

_____

_____

_____

Final Wrap-up

The road to victory is never found by taking the path of least resistance.

—Winston Churchill

CHAPTER
9

Reaching out to Others:
Especially Your Wife!

y husband just won't talk to me!" Kelly explained. "I
know he cares about me, but he just can't seem to express it very well."

Communication is the key to an effective marriage, yet some couples find it extremely difficult to express their true feelings to one another. The feelings are inside them, but they remain bottled up. Unexpressed love is often interpreted as no love at all. In some cases, it may even be perceived as resentment or rejection.

Brian and Kelly had been married for three years. There were no major problems on the surface of their marriage. But there was plenty of frustration underneath. They tried to talk about it, but they inevitably ended up in confused silence.

"One of you has to be willing to reach out to the other one," I suggested. "It will take courage and commitment to try, but you can't go on in silence."

"I'm willing," Kelly said. "But what if he doesn't respond?"

"You're not the first woman to face that concern," I replied. "Ruth did it, and it worked for her!"

The little Book of Ruth is like a ray of sunshine at the end of a long, dark tunnel. It was originally part of the Book of Judges. It was the only ray of hope after 300 years of failure and heartache. Just when it seemed everything was going wrong, God reminded His people that He was still protecting the promise.

On the surface, the promise seemed more obscure than ever. God was not worshiped. His law was not obeyed. And His Messiah had not come forth. It appeared to many that there was little hope for the future.

Life was dim when Elimelech ("God is my King") and Naomi ("pleasant one") left Bethlehem because of a famine. "Surely things will be better in Moab," they thought. So off they went with their two sons, Mahlon ("sickly") and Kilion ("pining"), to live among Israel's enemies, the Moabites.

Moab was a strange place to find a better life. It was populated by people who had long opposed Jehovah in favor of other gods. Moabites were notorious for their pagan rituals, including child sacrifice. It was hardly the place to start a new beginning.

When Everything Goes Wrong

While they were in Moab, Elimelech died. Eventually Mahlon and Kilion married Moabite girls named Ruth and Orpah. They seemed happy at first, but both of the boys soon died as well. In just ten short years, Naomi lost her husband and both of her sons.

The Book of Ruth is written like a four-act play. As the curtain goes up on scene one, we see three widows crying together in the fields of Moab. Broken and destitute, Naomi announced to them that she was returning home to Bethlehem.

"Go back, each of you, to your mother's home," she suggested to her daughters-in-law. "May the LORD show kindness to you.... May the LORD grant that each of you will find rest in the home of another husband" (Ruth 1:8,9).

Life was hard for widows in those days. They had no security, no income, and no means of working. Survival was all they could hope for. There were no welfare programs for the poor. Their only real hope was that their relatives would take them back.

Naomi's suggestion seemed reasonable to Orpah. So she kissed Naomi good-bye and returned to her family. But Ruth refused to leave her. She clung to her skirts.

The promise had to be fulfilled, and God specifically chose these two widows to keep it alive.

"Your sister-in-law is going back to her people and her gods," Naomi told her. "Go back with her" (1:15).

It was a desperate appeal by a desperate woman. Naomi realized what awaited them in Bethlehem: rejection, ridicule, and scorn.

But Ruth was determined to go with her. "Don't urge me to leave you or to turn back from you," she insisted. "Where you go I will go, and where you stay I will stay. Your people will be my people and your God my God. Where you die I will die, and there I will be buried. May the LORD deal with me... if anything but death separates you and me" (1:16,17).

What commitment! What an appeal! How could Naomi refuse? Ruth was more committed to her mother-in-law than some husbands and wives are to each other. There was an inseparable bond between them. Together they headed down the road on their way to an appointment with destiny.

Starting Over

The promise had to be fulfilled, and God specifically chose these two widows to keep it alive. There were no spectacular fireworks—just a daughter-in-law's love. But that was all God needed. He could take care of the rest. The Promisor would sustain the promise.

When they arrived in Bethlehem, the whole town came out to meet them. It was quite a spectacle—a Jewish woman with a Moabite daughter-in-law. Racial prejudice isn't anything new. It's been around a long time.

"Can this be Naomi?" the older women asked. It wasn't easy hiding your age in those days. Time had left its mark on her wrinkles, gray hair, and all the rest.

"Don't call me Naomi ['Pleasant']," she lamented. "Call me Mara" ['bitter']. . . . The LORD has afflicted me; the Almighty has brought misfortune upon me" (Ruth 1:20,21).

Naomi's new name indicates that she was a broken woman. She surely would have known the Lord's instructions to His people about not forsaking their inheritance. They were supposed to keep their land in the family as a gift from God. But she and Elimelech had done otherwise. They had sought their fortune in Moab and lost everything.

Like many husbands, Elimelech probably suggested that they could do better elsewhere. So they forsook the security of family and friends and struck out on their own. It is obvious from the scant information we have that things did not go well for them. Tragedy strikes only three verses into the first chapter. Before long, Naomi had no male protection for herself or the girls. "At least in Bethlehem, our relatives might take pity on us," she probably thought.

Ruth and Naomi arrived in Bethlehem during the barley harvest and found a relative's house to lodge in. It wasn't much, but it was still a new beginning. It was at least a chance to catch their breath and to start over again.

Time Out

1. *Have you ever lost everything dear and wondered what God was trying to say to you?*

2. *What lessons did you eventually learn?*

Times Have Changed

There are two concepts that underlie the Book of Ruth. The first is *theological.* It is the concept of the kinsman-redeemer. The kinsman-redeemer was a relative who could potentially redeem you with money from three basic conditions:

1. Slavery: Set you free.
2. Widowhood: Marry you as his wife.
3. Orphanhood: Adopt you as his child.

The second concept is *social.* It is the practice of levirate marriage (cf. Deuteronomy 25:5). Levirate marriage involved permission for a widow to marry her deceased husband's closest available brother or cousin. This was done to preserve the seed of the deceased. It provided a way for his line of descent to continue. And it also provided security for the younger widows who could not fully support themselves.

Both concepts, the kinsman-redeemer and levirate marriage, are key to understanding the Book of Ruth. As a widow, Ruth desperately needed to find a relative of her husband who would marry her and redeem her from widowhood. However, since she was a Moabite, her chances of acceptance by an Israelite were fairly slim.

The harvest was in full production. There was plenty of grain in Bethlehem ("house of bread"). So Ruth volunteered to go gleaning in the fields. The gleaners followed the reapers, who actually harvested the crops. Since harvesting was done by hand, a few scraps of grain naturally fell to the ground. That's where the gleaners came in: They picked up the scraps.

Gleaning was, in a sense, Israel's welfare program. Poor people were allowed to glean the leftover scraps of grain from the fields. But they had to work hard in order to eat. At the day's end, a gleaner might have only a handful of grain.

So Ruth picked a field to glean and began following the reapers. By chance, she chose a field that belonged to Boaz, a wealthy man from Bethlehem. She didn't know who he was or even where she was. She simply worked alongside the other girls throughout the morning.

A Date with Destiny

As the day wore on, Boaz came out from Bethlehem to inspect the harvest. "The Lord be with you!" he called to the harvesters.

"The Lord bless you!" they shouted back.

Then he saw her. A Gentile girl. A Moabite. Gleaning in his field. If there was ever a story of love at first sight, this would be it.

"Whose young woman is that?" he asked the foreman.

"She is the Moabitess who came back from Moab with Naomi," the foreman explained nervously. He went on to explain why he had let her out there. But no need for that. Boaz was already interested.

His heart pounding within him, he hurried over to meet the girl. "Listen to me," he said. "Don't go and glean in another field.... Stay here with my servant girls. Watch the field where the men are harvesting, and follow along after the girls. I have told the men not to touch you" (Ruth 2:8,9).

Ruth was overwhelmed by his generosity. She bowed her face to the ground and asked, "Why have I found such favor in your eyes that you notice me—a foreigner?" (2:10).

He explained to her that he had heard how she had come to Bethlehem with her mother-in-law, and what a blessing she had been to her. He also mentioned that he had heard how she had come to believe in the Lord and now sought refuge among His people.

Overcoming the Barriers

Here we see a Jewish man and a Gentile girl conversing in the fields of Bethlehem. Both are reaching beyond the social, religious, and cultural barriers that should have separated them. Nevertheless, Boaz showed grace to Ruth, and her heart was moved. She probably blushed as she spoke to him. He was famous in Bethlehem. He was one of the city's most outstanding men. And he was single!

"May the Lord repay you for what you have done," Boaz suggested.

"May I continue to find favor in your eyes, my lord," Ruth replied.

It was the beginning of an incredible romance. Love at first sight. It can happen, you know. At least, it did for them.

When Ruth returned to glean, Boaz instructed the foreman to let her glean even among the sheaves (standing grain). In fact, he suggested they drop some handfuls of grain on purpose for her to glean. Now that was true love—handfuls on purpose! She gathered a bushel basket full on the first day. She had so much that she could hardly carry it home.

Naomi couldn't believe her eyes. It was enough grain for a month! "Where did you glean today?" she asked.

"The name of the man I worked with today is Boaz," Ruth explained.

This time Naomi couldn't believe her ears. "The Lord bless him!" she shouted. "That man is our close relative; he is one of our kinsman-redeemers" (Ruth 2:20).

Naomi knew what this could mean, even though Ruth didn't. It was too good to be true. The finest and wealthiest man in all Bethlehem had taken notice of the Gentile girl. Could it be that he might be interested in redeeming her?

Halftime

1. *Have you ever been willing to reach out to someone across racial or social boundaries?*

2. *Could those people you reached say they truly found favor or grace in your actions?*

Some Things Never Change

Ruth continued gleaning in Boaz's fields until the harvest was over. As the weeks passed, she and Naomi began to wonder if he would ever make a move to show his interest toward her. When Boaz didn't make a move, Naomi decided Ruth should make one. She advised Ruth to go to him and propose marriage.

"Is that really in the Bible?" a single woman asked me.

"It sure is!" I replied. "Read Ruth, chapter 3. It worked for her."

Naomi realized time was running out. The harvest would soon be over. The time for action was now.

"Tonight he will be winnowing barley on the threshing floor," Naomi observed.

When the harvest was nearly over, the landowner would come to oversee the winnowing process. That's when they threw the grain up into the wind to blow off the chaff. It was a long, slow process done with a scoop shovel. Naomi knew that Boaz would be exhausted by the end of the day. It was the perfect time to make their move!

"Wash and perfume yourself," the Jewish mother told her Moabite daughter-in-law. "And put on your best clothes" (Ruth 3:3).

Some strategies never change! Old Naomi knew that Ruth would make a better impression all fixed up. Nothing like a bath, your best dress, and some perfume—"Midnight at the Oasis"—to knock him senseless.

And Boaz was probably exhausted from the day's labors. He has little energy to resist—even if he had wanted to.

"When he lies down...go and uncover his feet and lie down," Naomi instructed Ruth. "He will tell you what to do" (3:4).

It seems like a strange maneuver to us today, but it made perfect sense in their culture. The act of uncovering his feet was a deliberate proposal of marriage.

When Boaz awoke, startled to find a woman lying at his feet, Ruth said, "Spread the corner of your garment over me, since you are a kinsman-redeemer" (3:9).

She Proposes to Him

She was asking him to take her unto himself so that she might come under his protection. She appealed to him as her kinsman-redeemer (Hebrew, *goel*). Only a free man who was a close relative of her deceased husband could become her redeemer. He had to be:

1. Free
2. Single
3. Kinsman
4. Able to pay the price of redemption.
5. Willing to pay the price of redemption.

Boaz met all of these conditions, despite being somewhat older than Ruth. And he reassured her that he was willing to accept her proposal.

"The Lord bless you, my daughter," he said reassuringly.... "Don't be afraid. I will do for you all you ask.... You are a woman of noble character" (Ruth 3:10,11).

It was quite a testimony to her virtue, dignity, and character. He was impressed with her devotion to Naomi. And he was also impressed that she preferred him over the younger men.

However, there was one problem with the whole arrangement.

"Although it is true that I am near of kin," Boaz explained to Ruth, " there is a kinsman-redeemer nearer than I" (3:12).

Someone else! She couldn't bear the thought. But Boaz assured her he would try to work it out. He explained that he would have to meet with the other kinsman the next morning to clarify his right to redeem her.

"If he wants to redeem [you], good; let him redeem," Boaz added. "But if he is not willing, I vow that, as surely as the LORD lives, I will do it" (3:13).

Ruth could hardly contain herself when she returned home to Naomi. Boaz's words kept ringing in her ears. She wanted him, not the other one. He was the love of her soul. He was the one who extended grace and kindness to her, and her heart beat for him. The thought of losing him was more than she could bear.

"Wait, my daughter, until you find out what happens," Naomi advised. "For the man will not rest until the matter is settled today" (3:18). It was her way of reassuring Ruth that things would work out.

Have I Got a Deal for You

When the sun came up over Bethlehem, Boaz was already positioned at the city gate where all business was transacted in those days. Sooner or later, he knew the other kinsman would arrive. And sure enough, he shortly appeared.

"Come over here, my friend, and sit down," Boaz suggested. After a moment of greetings and chitchat, Boaz got right to the point. "Naomi . . . is selling the piece of land that belonged to our brother Elimelech" (Ruth 4:3).

In ancient Israel, land could only be sold to relatives within one's family. All land was viewed as a gift from God, or the "inheritance of the Lord." It could not be sold to strangers. Assuming the kinsman might want the land, Boaz informs him of his right to redeem it.

"I will redeem it," the kinsman announced.

But only then did Boaz explain that he would also have to redeem Ruth, the Moabitess. "On the day you buy the land from Naomi and from Ruth the Moabitess, you acquire the dead man's widow, in order to maintain the name of the dead with his property" (4:5).

The kinsman refused. He was willing to take the property but not the girl. "I cannot redeem it because I might endanger my own estate," he explained to Boaz. "You redeem it yourself. I cannot do it," he added (4:6).

By saying this, the first kinsman passed the right of redemption to Boaz. He was able to pay the price of redemption, but he was unwilling because of his previous commitment. He may well have been engaged to be married to someone else.

Building a successful marriage takes time, patience, energy, and determination.

"Today you are witnesses," Boaz told the city elders who had gathered with them in the gate. "I have also acquired Ruth the Moabitess, Mahlon's widow, as my wife" (4:9,10).

Then they exchanged sandals on the matter—another strange custom. It meant you were giving your word to keep the bargain. If you failed, the other man would wave your sandal in your face, reminding you that you could no longer walk among the people with honesty and integrity. It was like a receipt or bill of sale.

"We are witnesses," affirmed the city elders. "May the LORD make the woman who is coming into your home like Rachel and Leah, who together built up the house of Israel" (4:11).

They were referring to Jacob's wives, the mothers of the patriarchs. An interesting side note is the fact that Rachel had died centuries earlier right there in Bethlehem. And now Boaz, one of Leah's descendants through the tribe of Judah, was being blessed by Bethlehem's town fathers.

Building a successful marriage is a lifetime commitment. It takes time, patience, energy, and determination. The marks of an effective marriage include:

1. Lifelong commitment
2. Continual effort
3. Willingness to understand
4. Developing a helpful attitude
5. Consideration for your partner
6. Spiritual growth and maturity
7. Becoming genuinely unselfish
8. Personal accountability and reliability
9. Honest communication
10. Genuine, Spirit-filled love

Reaching out to each other says, "I care about you, I need you, and I want you." Every marriage needs that kind of effort if both partners want to know true fulfillment.

His Fame Is Our Fortune

Boaz and Ruth were setting out on one of the great adventures of life—building a family. Their love for each other initiated a marriage. But their commitment to each other initiated a family. And that family changed the course of history.

"May you have standing in Ephratah and be famous in Bethlehem," the elders shouted to Boaz. And indeed, he was! The redeemer had paid the price of redemption. The promise was secure. The line of the Messiah would be preserved.

Boaz, the wealthy Jew from Bethlehem, married Ruth, the Gentile widow from Moab. It was a wonderful marriage. And soon they were blessed with a child, whose name was Obed. Then the townswomen gathered around and said, "Praise be to the LORD, who this day has not left you without a kinsman-redeemer. May he become famous throughout Israel!" (Ruth 4:14).

One cannot read this powerful love story without making an obvious comparison. Bethlehem was the same little town that would give birth to another famous inhabitant: the Lord Jesus. Like Boaz, he too would become a Kinsman-Redeemer. Free from the enslavement of sin, able and willing to pay the price of redemption with His own blood, He would redeem us from spiritual slavery and set us free from orphanhood and adopt us as His children, free from widowhood, and make us His bride.

The Kinsman-Redeemer, wealthy with righteousness, would pay the price of our redemption. He would redeem a Gentile bride and make her His own. Born Himself of a virgin in Bethlehem, of the tribe of Judah and the seed of David, He is the Messiah—the ultimate fulfillment of the promise. And we are his undeserving bride who can only fall on our faces and ask, "Why have I found grace in your sight?"

Jesus, the Savior, loves you, and He wants to spend eternity with you.

Jesus, the Savior, came forth from Bethlehem to find us slaving over the scraps in the field of life. And He loved us in spite of our pitiful situation. He set his heart on us and promised, "I will marry you and redeem you." It is the pledge of the ultimate Redeemer to you and me personally. He loves you, and He wants to spend eternity with you.

We are the objects of His amazing grace. He has called us unto Himself and loved us with an everlasting love. What love! What hope! What security!

Postgame Highlights

1. Do I need to be willing to reach out to others?

2. Could I express my love for my wife better?

Personal Interview

Make a list of all the things you could do this week to demonstrate your love for your wife.

_____

_____

_____

_____

Final Wrap-up

Effective family life does not just happen;
it's the result of deliberate intention,
determination and practice.

–Chuck Swindoll

Realizing Your Goals:

Confidence in the Face of Danger

Location, location, location!" Today's real estate brokers shout it time and time again. They are trying to remind us that specific places are important in our decisions. The same is true in the Bible. There are many stories in the Bible that God uses to get our attention. They act as living illustrations of how He transforms ordinary men into great leaders of faith and victory. Some of these stories have such a tremendous impact on us that we never forget them. One such story is that of David's victory over Goliath. It is a story of faith and victory over incredible odds.

We find this story in 1 Samuel 17, which begins by telling us the location of this event: the Valley of Elah. To be precise, the part of the valley located between Socoh and Azekah, near Ephes Dammim. Those names aren't familiar to most people today, but they are real places. Just as real as Atlanta, Chicago, and Boston.

You can travel to Israel today and find the location of these ancient sites. You can actually stand in the very valley where David and Goliath had their historic confrontation. One of the greatest proofs that the Bible is true is the fact that the places it mentions are really there.

Our text goes on to explain that King Saul of Israel had assembled on the eastern hillside, while the Philistines lined up their army to the west. This was no ordinary Old Testament battle. This was a battle for the very existence of the nation of Israel. They had struggled against the Philistines for 200 years. A loss now would cost them everything.

> *One of the greatest proofs that the Bible is true is the fact that the places it mentions are really there.*

The people of Israel had grown tired of the struggle. They begged God to give them a king to fight their battles for them. God reminded them through the prophet Samuel that He was their king. But that wasn't good enough. They wanted a king they could see—one like the other nations had. So God told Samuel to make Saul their king since he was an "impressive young man without equal among the Israelites—a head taller than any of the others" (1 Samuel 9:2).

The only problem was that Saul did not have a heart for God. He was greedy, selfish, and jealous. His kingship was a failure, and his kingdom was about to collapse. The Promise was in jeopardy as well. No one had yet come on the scene to fulfill it. And the promised line was not on the throne.

Too Big to Miss

The time had come for God to expose Saul's weakness. He had some initial success battling Canaanites, Ammonites, and Amalekites. But these weren't "ites." They were "stines"–Philistines. Europeans. Greeks. Sea people. They had iron swords and spears. Israel was no match for them.

The Philistines kept the Israelites under their control by disarming them. At one point, only Saul and his son Jonathan had swords. The rest were fighting with farming tools (cf. 1 Samuel 13:19-22). But God is not limited to human instruments or human weapons. He had raised up Shamgar to defeat them with an oxgoad (Judges 3:31), and Samson with the jawbone of a donkey (Judges 15:15). So why not David with a sling?

The Israelites thought he was too big to hit. But David realized he was too big to miss!

Since Saul was taller than anyone in Israel, God sent him an enemy who was even taller: Goliath. The Bible describes the Philistine "giant" as being over nine feet tall. Proportionately, he would have weighed at least 600 pounds. He was huge! Big enough to be the entire front line of a football team. And he scared Saul and the Israelites to death.

Notice, however, that Goliath was *not* a "Jack-in-the-beanstalk" kind of giant who was 30 feet tall. He was a very real, very believable giant. He was big enough that the Israelites thought he was too big to hit. But David realized he was too big to miss!

Ed Dobson, pastor of Calvary Church in Grand Rapids, Michigan, is one of my closest lifelong friends. He recently shared an interesting observation about David and Goliath with me.

"I think most Christians are more like Goliath than David," he stated emphatically.

Now, that really got my attention. "What do you mean?" I asked.

"Look at Goliath!" he insisted. "He has *enormity*. He's over nine feet tall. He has *equipment*—over 100 pounds of armor, plus his weapons. And he has *experience*. He is a man of war."

Then he went on to make an astute observation. "We often don't trust in God," he suggested. "We trust in our size, our budget, our high-tech equipment, our state-of-the-art programming, and our history and heritage."

It was quite an observation. The successful modern church is more like Goliath than David. Sometimes we trust everything but God to get the job done. Not David. He went out to face Goliath armed with faith in God. He dared to go where no one else would go. And he went with very little in his hands.

For 40 days, morning and evening, Goliath taunted the Israelites. "I defy the ranks of Israel!" he shouted. "Give me a man and let us fight each other" (1 Samuel 17:10).

Battle by Champions

Goliath was proposing a challenge that was very familiar to the Philistines' Greek heritage: battle by champions. The Greeks had followed this practice for centuries. Fight for a few days, then stop and send out two representatives—champions such as Ajax, Hercules, Hector, Achilles. Let them fight it out. That was how you could determine whom the gods had chosen to win.

The Israelites probably didn't understand the concept at all. They only believed in one God—Jehovah. Besides, if they sent out a representative, it would have been Saul. He was their king and their tallest warrior. But he wasn't about to volunteer himself.

The battle dragged on for 40 days (1 Samuel 17:16). Goliath issued his challenge 80 times, and no one ever responded. It was humiliating and demoralizing. The average Israelites probably thought, "I'm not going anywhere near that monster!"

Day after day and night after night, Goliath issued his challenge: "Settle the conflict. Send out a champion!" Day after day and night after night–no takers!

In the meantime, back in Bethlehem, David's father, Jesse, became concerned about the welfare of his three oldest sons who were serving in the army with Saul. So he loaded up David with some provisions and sent him off to the battlefield.

"See how your brothers are, and bring back some assurance from them," Jesse called as David ran off with the sack of groceries.

Time Out

1. *What obstacles are you facing in your life right now?*

2. *Why is God allowing them, and what is He trying to teach you through them?*

Who Is This Kid?

It was a short jaunt over the hills to the Valley of Elah, especially for a 17 year old. David's legs churned as he flew over the rocky ledges to the valley's edge. He came up behind the Israelite camp early in the morning as the soldiers were preparing to start up the battle again that day.

The Bible describes the setting as follows: David "reached the camp as the army was going out to its battle positions, shouting the war cry" (1 Samuel 17:20). Imagine the excitement of this young teenager. A real live war was going on right before his eyes. Shields up. Swords flashing. Men running.

David ran right along with them—unarmed and carrying a bag of groceries. What a sight he was, screaming the war cry at the top of his lungs! The soldiers running beside him probably thought, "Who is this kid? And what's in that bag?"

About the time David found his brothers, he also discovered Goliath. He was the biggest thing David had ever seen! No wonder the Israelites fled from him in terror. He was big enough to crush a man to death. The entire Israelite army slowed to a stop.

Then Goliath put his hands to his mouth and shouted across the narrow valley, "Hey, over there, send out a man to fight me!"

It was the forty-first morning. The eighty-first challenge. But David was hearing it for the very first time.

"Who is this uncircumcised Philistine," he asked, "that he should defy the armies of the living God?" (verse 26).

That's when the whole picture changed. Unlike the Israelites who were concerned about their safety, David was concerned about the reputation of his God. Even his oldest brother, Eliab, couldn't talk him out of his resolve.

When Eliab accused him of leaving the family flock unattended, David accused him by responding, "Is there not a cause?" (verse 29, KJV).

David recognized that the cause and purpose of God were at stake. That's why he volunteered to fight Goliath. When God's cause is at stake, God's people should speak up! But it takes a real man to stand up when the stakes are high. Some men wilt under pressure. Others talk big but never do anything.

Faith in Action

David was unique. He knew God personally, and it showed. He spoke of God's activity in his life with total confidence that God would deliver this enemy into his hand as well. In fact, he spoke with so much assurance that his brother shut his mouth.

David might as well have said, "You mean the cause of God is at stake here, and you did not speak up? Wait till I tell Dad! You're the eldest representative of our family, and you didn't volunteer! Shame on you! Wait until the old man hears about this!"

Eliab just stood there in stupid silence, like he had been hit by a bolt of lightning.

Somebody ran to King Saul and told him they had found a volunteer to fight Goliath.

"Send him here," Saul insisted, expecting one of the warriors. Instead, it was an unarmed teenager with a bag of groceries!

"Let no one lose heart on account of this Philistine," David said, trying to reassure the king. "Your servant will go and fight him" (1 Samuel 1:32).

Saul nearly had a heart attack himself. "You are not able to go out against this Philistine and fight him; you are only a boy" (verse 33).

A boy! David probably thought. *When are you people going to let me grow up!* "God helped me kill a lion and bear. And I can take this Philistine, too!"

David was so convincing that he talked Saul down. The kid had so much faith in God, the old king was stunned. Nobody talked like that anymore! David's faith in God was so real that it silenced his critics. Eliab was speechless. And now Saul was dumbfounded.

"He has defied the living God!" David insisted, as if to say, "He's the one who's in big trouble here, not me!"

David showed every essential quality of leadership. He knew what to do and how to do it, and he had the confidence to make it happen. Genuine leaders:

1. Build trust.
2. Set the example.
3. Facilitate high standards.
4. Develop a solid reputation.
5. Get the job done.

What's in Your Hand?

The amazing thing about the story of David is that Saul let him go. After all, he had nothing to lose. They had been fighting over this valley for 40 days. Saul was desperate. His army had to be discouraged. It was only a matter of time until they were beaten. "Besides," he may have thought, "who says we have to surrender if the kid gets killed?"

"Go, and the LORD be with you," Saul told David (verse 37). He may as well have said, "And I hope you don't get killed too badly!"

Saul offered David his armor, but the young man refused it. He didn't even know how it worked. Instead, he decided to go against Goliath with two things he had already brought with him: his shepherd's staff and his sling.

God will never put more in your hand until you are willing to use what is already there.

The staff was a long stick with a crook in the end of it. The sling was a leather pouch with two strands of leather attached to it. It was a weapon, not a toy slingshot, but it wasn't much of a weapon against Goliath. However, a kid with a good sling could throw a rock a hundred yards. I've watched Bedouin kids in Israel knock tin cans off a wall at that distance.

When David headed off to meet Goliath, he went with what he already had in his hands: the staff and the sling. He didn't ask God to put more in his hands before answering the challenge. Most of us never get going for God because we want Him to equip us first. We want a great voice before we will sing or speak for Him. We want great wealth before we will give to Him. We even want great courage before we will stand up for Him.

It doesn't work that way. God will never put more in your hand until you are willing to use what is already there. If you won't use what you have, why should He trust you with more? David went out with a staff in one hand and a sling in the other. Later, God put the scepter of Israel in his hand and the crown of king on his head because he had been willing to get started with what he had.

Halftime

1. *What do you already have in your "hand" that God wants to use?*

2. *When are you going to step out by faith and use it?*

Standing Alone

David walked alone out of the Israelite camp and down the hillside toward the brook of Elah. It still meanders along the bottom edge of the valley today. And it's still full of stones. When he got to the bottom of the hill, David picked five smooth stones out of the brook and put them in his shepherd's pouch.

I have stood in that same creek bed on numerous occasions—both when there was water in it and when there wasn't. Once you step up out of it, you are on the flat surface of the valley floor. The rocky cliff is behind you, and the tree-lined hills to the west are ahead of you.

The valley itself is no more than a mile wide. One can easily see and hear across it. And there, in that empty valley, walked a lone figure headed toward the Philistine encampment. David the shepherd boy—the future king of

Israel. The kid from Bethlehem. The son of the promise. The ancestor of the Messiah!

Goliath got excited. Someone had finally answered his challenge. He grabbed his sword and spear, and the shield-bearer moved out ahead of him. But when Goliath got closer, he saw that it was an unarmed teenager coming against him. The Bible says that the Philistine warrior despised David and laughed at him with scorn.

"Am I a dog, that you come at me with sticks?" he taunted (verse 43). Then he cursed David and promised to kill him and feed his flesh to the buzzards.

David had not been there those other days to listen to Goliath curse the God of Israel. He had not seen the army of Israel cower in fear. He had not seen Saul's weakness as their leader, nor their panic at the sight of Goliath. David was undeterred by all of that. He was on a mission. He was defending the cause of God.

"You come against me with sword and spear and javelin," he shouted back at Goliath, "but I come against you in the name of the LORD Almighty [Yahweh sabaoth], the God of the armies of Israel, whom you have defied. This day the LORD will hand you over to me.... Today I will give the carcasses of the Philistine army to the birds of the air... and the whole world will know that there is a God in Israel" (verses 45,46).

David wasn't after just Goliath. He intended to take on the entire Philistine army! Goliath stood there speechless. He hadn't heard any Israelites talk like this before. He hadn't seen such a display of faith and courage before. So he stayed to fight.

Total Abandonment

As Goliath lumbered toward him, David did something surprising—he ran right for him! There was no turning back now—no potshots from behind a boulder. David totally abandoned himself to God. *Here I go, live or die. You'd better be there!* he may have thought.

David reached into his bag on a dead run, pulled out a stone, put it in the sling, wound up, and threw it right at Goliath's head. The stone rose from the underhanded motion of the sling, cleared the shield, and struck Goliath right in the forehead. It killed him instantly. His huge body came crashing to the ground with an incredible thud. Silence fell across the valley. Philistines and Israelites alike were stunned. "He's down!" they muttered.

David stood alone with God in that valley. He left the faithless and fearful army of Israel behind. He left his brothers behind. He even left King Saul behind. And in that one incredible moment, he became Israel's greatest hero. When he left home, he was a shepherd boy. By midmorning, he was a national hero.

There was something very unusual about David. He had a deep and personal faith in God. He stood out from all the rest. His was no textbook faith. It was the kind of faith that one could live by or die for.

When David left home, he had no idea what lay ahead of him. He got up just like he did every other day. But this day would be different. This day he would step out by faith and abandon all he had to God. He left home a boy, but he returned a man.

Standing Tall

Once Goliath hit the ground, David was the only one left standing tall on the battlefield. He upstaged everybody that day—his brother, Saul, Goliath, the Israelites, and even the Philistines. In less than one hour, he alone had done what the army of Israel hadn't been able to do for 40 days.

Then David did something only a teenager would do. He ran up to the fallen body of Goliath. The King James Version says he "stood upon" it. I can just see him walking all over the dead body. He probably thought, *Wow! Look at this thing. It's huge!*

Next, he took Goliath's own sword and cut off his head. Then he stood up with the head in his hands. And when the Philistines saw it, they fled for their lives. David didn't even need the other four stones he had picked up in the brook. One killed Goliath and sent the entire Philistine army into retreat.

There are no easy roads to victory. It takes faith and courage to face the obstacles of life.

Finally, the Israelites pursued them. They waited until David had killed Goliath and put the Philistines to flight. Then, the Bible says, they chased them back to the gates of Ekron. Not only had David done in an hour what the army couldn't do in a month, but he also accomplished something in one day that the whole nation of Israel hadn't done in a hundred years: defeated the Philistines in battle.

There are no easy roads to victory. It takes faith and courage to face the obstacles of life. But the spoils of victory do not go to the weak or fainthearted. The victory goes to those whose faith exceeds the obstacles. Those who dare to dream the impossible dream. Those who reach for the unreachable. They are the real winners.

Keys to personal victory include:

1. *Attitude.* Positive people are the best achievers. Negative people eventually give up and lose.
2. *Analysis.* Decision-makers get the facts, analyze the facts, and decide what to do quickly. They reject "analysis paralysis."
3. *Action.* Winners take action. They refuse to be victims. They decide what to do and do it. If they run into obstacles, they deal with them and keep moving.

What will it take to see our nation turn back to God? Hundreds? Thousands? No! It will only take a few Davids willing to stand alone for God. Men of faith who will abandon themselves to the cause and purpose of God. Men who are willing to surrender their agendas to God. Men who will put God first in their lives.

Revival always has a price tag. It costs the sacrifice of ourselves to God. For some, it will mean giving up habits and practices that do not glorify God. For some, it will mean sacrificing our time and energy to serve God. For others, it will mean putting your wife and family ahead of your career. It will always mean reordering your priorities to bring them in line with God's priorities.

Ask yourself, Is God really first in my spiritual life, marriage, family, business, goals, finances, time, and activities? You will never experience the kind of revival that can revolutionize your family and friends until you experience it changing you. Real revival is both personal and life-changing.

David became a great leader because he knew God personally. The Bible calls him a "man after God's heart." He overcame great obstacles to become Israel's greatest king. He later fled from Saul's jealous animosity. But he eventually returned to take the kingdom, write the psalms, and become the leader of Israel's worship of God. As the great-grandson of Ruth and Boaz, David finally brings the promise to its initial fulfillment. There is indeed hope for the future.

Postgame Highlights

1. *Where do you need to be willing to stand alone for God?*

2. *What is holding you back from making a total surrender to Him?*

Personal Interview

List all the areas of your life where you need to be victorious:

_____

_____

_____

_____

_____

_____

Final Wrap-up

Weak leaders stay within safe boundaries.
Great leaders march off the map!

—Alexander the Great

CHAPTER

11

Developing Lasting Friendships:

Value of True Loyalty

Friendships are made. They don't just happen. Real friendships need time to grow. And growth comes with depth in communication. You can build only surface relationships with surface conversations. You have to reach beyond the small talk in order to build bridges to other people.

"Hi! How are you?" we ask.

"Fine," they reply.

Soon the whole process becomes a ritual. After a while, all you have to do is say, "Hi," and people will automatically respond, "Fine." You don't even have to ask how they are! They just say "fine" out of habit, whether they are fine or not.

If we are not careful, all of our conversations at work or church can degenerate into a whole series of clichés:

"How's it going?"

"Great!"

"Nice day we're having."

"Couldn't be better."

"How 'bout them Cowboys?"

"Man, that's really something!"

"Don't do anything I wouldn't do."

"Keep up the good work."

"Say 'hi' to your wife and kids."

"See you in church."

Even the handshaking ritual in most of our churches fails to promote any real communication between people. We turn, smile, shake hands, say "hello," and move on to the next person. Then we start it all over again.

How many times has your wife asked, "Who is that guy you were talking to?" And your response was, "I'm really not sure what his name is."

The same thing happens with most people at work. We see the same faces day after day, pass by, say "hi," and keep on going. We don't really know who they are, where they came from, or what they're all about.

True friendships take time to develop. Many times we have to overcome our initial impressions of people to build relationships with them. This happened to my wife and I when we moved to St. Louis a few years ago. One of the couples in our new Bible class really stood out.

Getting Past the Obvious

Connie, a middle-aged wife and mother, had a spiked hairdo! You might describe it as the "ultra-contemporary look." But the truth was, you couldn't miss it if you tried! Her husband, Terry, on the other hand, seemed quiet and unassuming. He looked more like the all-American type.

A few weeks later, I was walking through the St. Louis airport, when a voice called out to me.

"Hey, Ed! I'm Terry Goodin. My wife and I are in your Sunday school class."

"Terry Goodin," I thought. "Oh, yeah, he's the guy whose wife has that weird hairdo!"

"Are you in a hurry to catch a plane?" Terry asked.

"Actually, my flight has been delayed," I replied. "I've got an hour to kill."

"Would you like to get a cup of coffee?" Terry suggested.

"Sure," I responded habitually.

We went into the little cafeteria at the airport and sat and talked while we sipped our coffee. Soon, we learned that we were both new in town and that our kids were the same ages.

That brief meeting signaled the beginning of a lifelong friendship. Our kids became good friends, which drew us together as families. Ironically, we had little else in common. Terry was into computers. I was in ministry. Connie was spontaneous and outgoing. And Donna was quiet and reserved.

The older you get, the more you realize how important your friends are to you.

But the friendship clicked despite our differences. The blend was just right. We laughed and talked and thoroughly enjoyed each other's company. There is a chemistry to these kinds of friendships. We were all different enough to really appreciate each other. But we were also drawn together by our mutual commitment to Christ.

Terry and Connie have a real heart for God. So our friendship was an opportunity for all of us to grow. The relationship our children developed helped them grow as well. And to think we almost missed this blessing over a hairdo!

Eventually we moved to Atlanta, and the Goodins moved to Phoenix. Terry took a job with one of the major computer companies. But we still keep in touch and visit back and forth. Time and distance seem to strengthen our friendship. As soon as we are together, it's like old times again.

The older you get, the more you realize how important your friends are to you. As the kids grow up and leave home, you will find yourself valuing your time with your friends more and more.

Lifelong Friends

David and Jonathan became lifelong friends as soon as they met. They had a lot in common. They were both courageous warriors. When Jonathan saw David kill Goliath, he was instantly drawn to him. The Bible says, "Jonathan became one in spirit with David" (1 Samuel 18:1).

Jonathan's father was King Saul. Inept as he was, Saul wasn't about to let the victorious David get away. He drafted him into the Israelite army and gave him a position of command. The unarmed teenager was now an unarmed commander. The Bible says that Jonathan was so impressed with David that he gave him his own robe, his own sword, and his own bow (18:4).

David was immediately successful as Israel's new champion. And the two young men became inseparable friends. But David's success soon made Saul jealous. Actually, he was afraid of David because the Lord's hand was upon him. When he couldn't get rid of him, Saul decided to marry his daughter Michal to David to keep close tabs on him. That made Jonathan David's brother-in-law.

Despite David's rocky marriage to his sister and the animosity of his father, Jonathan remained David's loyal friend. When Saul ordered Jonathan to kill David, he protested and defended David's innocence. He was even temporarily able to secure a truce between his father and David (cf. 1 Samuel 19:4-7).

Unfortunately, Saul's good disposition did not last long. David's continued military success only frustrated the old king all the more. He tried to have David assassinated at home, but Michal helped him escape. David ran to the prophet Samuel for refuge at Ramah. Then he went to Jonathan and asked him to intervene on his behalf.

"What have I done? What is my crime?" David pleaded to Jonathan. "How have I wronged your father, that he is trying to take my life?" (1 Samuel 20:1).

"It's not so!" Jonathan insisted.

"Your father doesn't want you to know about this," David implied. "There is only a step between me and death."

Realizing the danger David was facing, Jonathan promised to help him. "Whatever you want me to do, I'll do for you," he said (20:4).

David asked Jonathan to find out how Saul really felt about him. A special festival was being celebrated the next day, and they both knew David would be missed if he did not show up. So Jonathan promised to intervene for him and to bring him word of his father's response in two days.

The young men agreed to meet at a certain spot near the rock Ezel. Jonathan explained that he would shoot three arrows beside the stone. Then he would send out a boy to fetch them. They planned if he told the boy to "bring the arrows here," all was safe for David to return. But if he told the boy the arrows are "beyond you," David should run away.

When David didn't show up at the festival, Saul blew up. And when Jonathan tried to defend David, Saul blew up at him.

"You son of a perverse and rebellious woman!" the king shouted.

Then Saul berated Jonathan for defending David: "As long as the son of Jesse lives on this earth, neither you nor your kingdom will be established. Now send and bring him to me, for he must die!" (20:31).

That did it! Jonathan stormed out in a rage, yet grieved over his father's shameful behavior.

Time Out

1. *Who are your closest friends?*

2. *Has a friendship ever led you to sacrifice your own well-being?*

There's Nothing Like a Crisis

Crises have a way of cementing lifelong friendships. When you go through deep waters together, your hearts pull together more than ever. Ed Dobson and Vernon Brewer are my two closest lifelong friends. I've known them both since they were in their early twenties. We have traveled together, preached together, prayed together, and wept together. We have shared the best of times and the worst of times.

Ed and Vernon have always been there every time I needed them. Even though we are separated by many miles, time and distance have not diminished our relationship. The first time I met Ed, he was a graduate student. Upon first impression, he seemed arrogant and conceited. But I would later learn that his confidence was in God, not in himself. When I heard him preach for the first time, I was struck with his natural and spiritual gifts as a great communicator of God's Word.

Crises have a way of cementing lifelong friendships

Vernon and I met around the same time. I was traveling with Life Action, a revival team, and he met us in Sarasota, Florida, to write a story about our ministry for a Christian magazine. He was bold, brash, and witty. He didn't walk into rooms in those days—he "exploded" into them! You couldn't miss him: plaid coat, red tie, loud voice.

Years later, we all worked together at Liberty University in Lynchburg, Virginia. We shared every kind of experience you could imagine: excitement, success, failure, crisis, conflict, sickness, and death. Some are just memories now, but I will never forget the one afternoon the phone rang.

"Vernon and Patti are at the hospital," Donna said with an urgency in her voice. "I think they want you and Ed to come right away."

Ed Dobson and I raced over to the hospital. Vernon had been sick, but he was always catching something, running all over the world like he did. There had been some concern about his cough not going away, but nothing more.

As we walked into the room where he was lying on the bed, we could see that awful look on his face. It was a blank stare of shocked unbelief. It was unlike any expression I had ever seen on him before.

"Well guys, it's the Big C," he announced as he sat up in bed. "They think I've got cancer... a tumor... right here in my chest."

Vernon took Patti's hand as he explained what the doctor had told him. We both hugged him and prayed with them. It was the beginning of a long and difficult journey. He had to have surgery immediately. His voice was badly damaged in the process. Months of chemotherapy followed. There was an accident at the outpatient clinic, and his hand was severely burned by the chemo. More surgery followed.

The next few months dragged on like an eternity. At times it seemed there was no end in sight. But eventually, he recovered. The surgeons repaired his hand and his voice. And in time, he was back to normal. He even looked like his old self–until he took his shirt off. Then he looked like he had been in a sword fight and lost!

God eventually led all three of us in different directions. But something had taken place during those difficult days. We had all joined together in an inseparable bond that still exists today. Lasting friendships are like that–deep and solid.

Don't Forget Me

Jonathan realized that he might never see David again. Yet he loved him too much to let his own father destroy him. He met David by the rock as he had promised. Then he shot the arrows and shouted, "Hurry! Go quickly! Don't stop!"

After the boy picked up the arrows, Jonathan gave him his weapons and sent him back to town. Unarmed, he proceeded to meet with David. They embraced each other and wept, David sobbing the hardest.

"Go in peace," Jonathan said, "for we have sworn friendship with each other in the name of the LORD" (1 Samuel 20:42).

They promised to always remain friends and even to bless each other's families. It was a promise with enormous consequences for the future, for they would see each other only once more.

Halftime

1. *Think of the most difficult times you have been through with your friends.*

2. *How did these times bond you together?*

A Tribute to a Friend

David spent years running from Saul. The paranoid king chased him all over the desert. But time and time again, David managed to escape because God was with him. At one point, he and Jonathan met secretly at Horesh in the Desert of Ziph (1 Samuel 23:15-18).

Jonathan tried to encourage his distraught friend. "Don't be afraid," he said. "My father Saul will not lay a hand on you. You will be king over Israel, and I will be second to you. Even my father Saul knows this" (23:17).

It was quite an admission from Jonathan. He was willing to give up his claim to the throne for his friend David. Now that is true friendship! Jonathan in essence was saying, "I want what is best for you, not just what is best for me."

Again they renewed their covenant, and again they parted company. In the meantime, Saul's pursuit of David continued. Twice David spared Saul's life. Nevertheless, Saul still continued his pursuit. Finally, in desperation, David escaped into the land of the Philistines to the city of Gath—Goliath's hometown.

As you might imagine, David had quite a reputation in Gath. Achish, the king of Gath, gladly made an alliance with him. At last, Saul gave up looking for David. However, things did not go back to normal; a double tragedy occurred. Not only did David and Jonathan never see each other again, but Jonathan was eventually killed in battle with his father by the hand of the Philistines (cf. 1 Samuel 31).

Friendships that last are the ones that grow in depth.

Saul's jealousy, pride, and paranoia cost him everything. He had turned against David and driven away the one man who could have saved him from the Philistines. In the end, Saul died in battle, and Jonathan died with him because of the sins of his father.

There was no rejoicing by David when news of their deaths reached him. His heart was broken for both Saul and Jonathan. He cried out:

> "How the mighty have fallen!... Saul and Jonathan... They were swifter than eagles, they were stronger than lions. O daughters of Israel, weep for Saul.... I grieve for you, Jonathan my brother; you were very dear to me. Your love for me was wonderful, more wonderful than that of women. How the mighty have fallen! (2 Samuel 1:19-27).

Bonds of Iron

It was quite a tribute to a lifelong friend. Eventually, David became the king of Israel, just as Jonathan had predicted. In the years to come, David showed kindness to Jonathan's family every opportunity he could—especially to his son Mephibosheth. The bonds of their friendship continued long after Jonathan's death. It was a deep, lasting relationship forged by the bond of human commitment.

Friendships that last are ones that grow in depth. There are at least four levels of friendship:

1. *Casual acquaintances.* We know their names and faces. We know them well enough to say "hello," but we rarely ever talk to them in any depth. We may know hundreds of such people.

2. *Casual friends.* We know them well enough to carry on a friendly conversation, but with very little depth. We might even chat with them over lunch, but we rarely open up to them. We may know scores of such people.

3. *Good friends.* Those people have interests and values similar to our own. We value their ideas and seek their opinions. We enjoy their company on a regular basis, but we are not necessarily lifelong friends. We may have a few dozen such friends.

4. *Intimate friends.* These are those few people with whom we have bonded deeply for life. They know all about us and like us in spite of our faults. We can and have shared our deepest joys, hurts, sorrows, blessings, and defeats with them. We love them and they love us.

Friendships are also developed around certain key ingredients:

1. Common interests: "We like the same things."

2. Personal significance: "You are important to me."
3. Honest communication: "Let me tell you the truth."
4. Unconditional love: "I like you the way you are."
5. Genuine concern: "I really care about you."
6. Personal encouragement: "I want what is best for you."
7. Long-term commitment: "Let's work through this."

When friendships contain these ingredients, they are bound to be successful. Whether they last a few years or an entire lifetime, such friendships are essential to our personal growth and emotional well-being. When the tough times come, God uses our friends to help us through. We all need friends we can rely on. Their help, advice, and encouragement are invaluable.

On the other hand, there are also friendships that can develop into negative relationships. They may begin in innocence, but somewhere along the way, they take a turn for the worse. *Negative relationships* have the following characteristics:

1. *Dependent.* When two friends become so overdependent on each other that they can't stand alone, make their own decisions, or live their own life.

2. *Possessive.* When one person controls the other by constant threats or demands. And he/she tries to isolate the other person from everyone else.

3. *Hidden agenda.* When someone is only pretending to be a friend because they want something the other person has or they want to misuse the other person.

4. *Codependent.* When both parties reinforce each other's wrong behavior enabling one another to continue on a self-destructive course.

5. *Avoidance of the truth.* When there is no real honesty. Every issue of disagreement is simply avoided.

Reaching Beyond Ourselves

Every time we reach out to befriend someone, there are certain risks involved: rejection, misunderstanding, obligations, and commitments. They might not like me. They might not understand me. Worse yet, they might want me to help them with something.

"I need to move a couple of things up to the attic," a friend recently explained. "Could you give me a hand Saturday?"

We all need friends we can rely on.

"Saturday? This Saturday?" I murmured. "Sure, what are friends for anyway!"

We've all done things for our friends: picked up their mail, mowed their grass, towed their car, watched their kids. Why? Because that's what friends are for. We become friends when we respond to needs.

People need people. That's what life is all about. God created us with a desire for personal relationships. Instead of avoiding people, we all need to learn how to reach out to people. Our words of encouragement, acts of kindness, and attitudes of acceptance communicate to people that we care about them.

We have all heard the old proverb: "He who would have friends must himself be friendly." That's how you get friends. If you reach out to enough people, some of them will reach back to you.

David and Jonathan are unique examples of an unusual friendship. Warriors with a heart for battle. Friends with a heart for each other. Brothers-in-law whose lives were torn apart by Saul's animosity, yet whose hearts and friendship sealed them together in a common quest—the preservation of the promise.

The line of the Messiah was preserved despite Saul's hatred for David. God soon made David the king of Israel and through him defeated the Philistines once and for all. The shepherd boy was finally on the throne as God had promised many years before.

The Ultimate Friend

When God chose to show His love for us, He sent His Son to reach out to us. In this case, He left His throne to come down to the level of common humanity. He came not in the royal robes of His superiority, but in the simple garb of a carpenter's son. What's more, He came to die for our sins so that He might bring us to God.

Romans 5:6-8 says, "You see, at just the right time, when we were still powerless, Christ died for the ungodly. Very rarely will anyone die for a righteous man, though for a good man someone might possibly dare to die. But God demonstrates his own love for us in this: While we were still sinners, Christ died for us."

Jesus is the greatest friend you could ever have. He loves you even more than you love yourself. He proved it when He gave Himself to die in your place. That is the heart of the gospel message: "While we were yet sinners, Christ died for us." God placed our sin upon Christ, and then poured out His judgment on Him.

When Jesus died on the cross, He died as our substitute. He took our place. And He took our punishment as well. That's why the Bible calls Him the Lamb of God. His death was the sacrificial atonement for our sins. Receiving Him as your personal Savior involves believing with your whole heart that He died for you personally. And it also involves making a wholehearted commitment of yourself to Him by faith.

That commitment is something each one of us needs to make for ourselves. You can't get to heaven on your parents' faith or your wife's faith. You must make that decision for yourself. The Scripture tells us, "For Christ died for sins once for all, the righteous for the unrighteous, to bring you to God" (1 Peter 3:18).

If you need a true friend who will stand by you for time and eternity, Jesus is the greatest friend you could ever have. Give Him your heart and soul today. He will never leave you or forsake you.

Postgame Highlights

1. Do you have any destructive friendships that need to be changed or dropped?

2. Is God really your best friend?

Personal Interview

List all those friends who are having a positive influence on your life:

_____

_____

_____

Final Wrap-up

Friends realize the right to criticize must
be earned even if their advice
is constructive in nature.

–James Dobson

CHAPTER
12

Standing Up for What You Believe:

Developing Masculine Determination

M ost teenagers would have given in! Daniel was only 15 when Jerusalem was captured by the Babylonians, and it would have been a frightening experience for any teenager. Tensions between Babylon and Jerusalem had been mounting for several years. Finally, the Babylonians sent Nebuchadnezzar himself to take the city.

David's kingdom had lasted for over 400 years. The line of Davidic kings remained on the throne in Jerusalem throughout those years. And with them the line of the Messiah had been preserved as well. The promise had been kept alive and well, not by the faithfulness of the kings but by the faithfulness of God.

There had been both good kings and evil kings. The kingdom had reached its zenith under David and Solomon between 1000–940 B.C. After Solomon's death, the northern tribes, led by Ephraim, pulled away to establish their own capital in Samaria. In 722 B.C. the northern kingdom fell to the Assyrians. Judah, the southern kingdom, fared much better under great kings such as Hezekiah and Josiah. But other kings were not as faithful as Hezekiah and Josiah. They did not obey God's commands or keep His laws. Time had now run out. God's judgment had come. And once again the promise seemed bleak.

In the summer of 605 B.C. the powerful general and crown prince of Babylon, young Nebuchadnezzar, marched against the City of David and defeated it. Nebuchadnezzar's initial victory over Jerusalem was fairly merciful. He allowed the city and the Temple to stand, but he decided to take a few select captives back to Babylon.

He chose some of the choice young men from the royal family and the nobility. These educated and sophisticated young men would be reprogrammed to serve in the royal palace at Babylon. They were assigned to instructors who would teach them the language and literature of the Babylonians.

In other words, they were going to look, talk, and act like Babylonians. They were even given Babylonian names. Everything possible was done to assimilate them into Babylonian culture and to break down their Hebrew heritage.

Among the captives were four young Hebrews about 15 years of age. Their names were Daniel, Hananiah, Mischael, and Azariah. Each name identified them with the God of Israel: El or Jehovah. So the Babylonians renamed them after the names of their gods Bel, Mardach, and Nego. We know them as Belteshazzar, Shadrach, Meshach, and Abednego.

Talk About Peer Pressure

There were other Hebrew boys taken captive and put through this same process of cultural reorientation. But these four are the only ones whose names we know because they were the only ones who stood up for their faith in God.

The others compromised. Why not? "When in Babylon, do as the Babylonians," or something like that. Besides, "it's not our fault we were taken captive." What did people expect them to do–get in more trouble? A guy could lose his head if he made the wrong move in a place like this! After all, they had been kidnapped by a Middle Eastern dictator–a real mad man.

Talk about peer pressure! These young Jews were facing a life-or-death situation. They either had to compromise their beliefs or give up their lives. The choice was simple for most of them: Compromise, man, compromise!

Ancient Babylon is part of modern-day Iraq. We've all seen the video replay of Saddam Hussein patting the little British boy on the head while flashing a fake smile at the cameras. "Nice boy. You'll be safe here."

Yeah, sure! Heads are rolling. Bullets are flying. Bombs are dropping. People are being assassinated. Executions are a daily occurrence. Oh, yeah! Great place to go to school. I can't wait to see what final exams are like! If you don't pass, you end up shoveling sand in the desert!

That's exactly what being in Babylon in 605 B.C. was all about. Times haven't changed all that much over there. These teenagers were prisoners of war, and they knew it. In fact, they were royal hostages. They were being kept in Babylon as insurance against any further rebellion back home.

A Little Compromise Can't Hurt

There was one significant difference back then: Babylon was the greatest city on earth! It was the crown jewel of the Middle East. Its opulence exceeded any place on earth during this era. Its azure blue and sparkling gold walls glistened in the desert sun. It was the greatest metropolis in the whole world–a giant oasis in the middle of the desert.

Babylon sparkled with every kind of material attraction and personal temptation you could imagine. Being taken there was like being hauled off to Las Vegas. Every kind of enticement existed to appeal to their teenage senses. Besides, their parents were back in Jerusalem. Who would ever know if they gave in to a little temptation?

"A little compromise can't hurt, can it?" they may have asked. And from what we can tell from the Book of Daniel, most of them probably gave in to it. But notice that their names and their memories have long since been forgotten.

We remember only the heroes. The men and women of character are never forgotten.

That's how life is, you know. We remember only the heroes. The men and women of character are never forgotten. Somehow their lives make such an impression on us that we remember them long after they are gone.

The morally weak and spiritually deficient, on the other hand, are soon forgotten. Oh, we notice them while they are alive. But soon after they are gone, we erase them. Their self-centered lives are not worth remembering. Men of character are a different breed. They stand up for what they believe. And they stand out from the crowd.

The boys were assigned to a three-year training program similar to a modern university education. They would learn the intricacies of Babylonian art, science, mathematics, and religion. They were also assigned a portion of food and wine from the king's table. It was good stuff. The only problem was that it was considered unclean by Jewish standards.

What were they going to do? If they ate the food, they would be violating their religious convictions. But to refuse it meant refusing the king's provisions, which could cost you your head!

Time Out

1. *What pressures of compromise do you face in your life?*

2. *What are you doing to resist the pressure to give in?*

Dare to Be a Daniel

Daniel's name has long been associated with taking a stand for faith in God. In fact, Westminster Academy in St. Louis, Missouri, gives a "Daniel award" every year to the senior who most exemplifies standing up for his or her faith.

I will never forget sitting in the audience at Westminster's commencement in 1990, when our daughter Christy was called to the platform to win that award. My wife, Donna, just glowed! Christy winning the "Daniel award" meant more to Donna as a mother than all the other awards and honors given that day.

Our little Christy had become a young lady with a heart for God, and it showed. She had learned to stand up for Jesus Christ even amid the pressure of her peers. And she has been doing it ever since. Moving to St. Louis had been a challenge for all of us. But it was obvious that day that she was handling it just fine.

Daniel and his friends had a serious decision to make: They either had to accept the king's request or find a way to resist it. Rather than becoming defiant, the Bible says, "Daniel resolved not to defile himself" (Daniel 1:8). Then Daniel came up with a creative alternative. He asked the steward to exempt him and his friends from the requirement.

"I am afraid of my lord the king," the steward responded. "The king would then have my head because of you" (verse 10).

"Please test your servants for ten days," Daniel requested. "Give us nothing but vegetables to eat and water to drink. Then compare our appearance with that of the young men who eat the royal food" (verses 12,13).

It was a good idea. It gave the boys an option, and it gave the steward an option as well. "What harm could a little 'test' do?" the steward probably thought. "Ten days? All right! But only ten days!"

Putting Your Faith to the Test

The request meant that Daniel and his friends were putting their faith to the ultimate test. Meat and wine were normally dedicated to the idols and gods of pagan religions. Besides, Jewish dietary laws about such foods were very strict: no pork, only certain kinds of beef or chicken. Everything had to be kosher by Jewish standards.

The boys' request was intended to allow them to participate in their schooling without compromising their beliefs. It wasn't just a request to become vegetarians. The vegetables were certainly good for them, but they didn't require the same kind of kosher restrictions that meats did according to Jewish law.

At the end of ten days, the Bible says, "they looked healthier and better nourished than any of the young men who ate the royal food" (Daniel 1:15). So the steward allowed them to stay on their diet throughout the three-year training program.

At the end of the three years, the final examination was given by Nebuchadnezzar himself. Imagine the pressure! The powerful king personally asked the oral exam questions. They had better know the answers!

The Scripture says, "God gave knowledge and understanding of all kinds of literature and learning" to these four young men (1:17). The king examined them all and "found none equal to Daniel, Hananiah, Mishael and Azariah....In every matter of wisdom and understanding...he found them ten times better" (1:19,20).

God helped them to pass the examination because they stood up for their beliefs and convictions. One cannot read the Book of Daniel without being impressed by the character and courage of these young men. While they were still in the training program, Daniel interpreted Nebuchadnezzar's prophetic dreams and rose to a position of prominence. He and his friends were eventually appointed to be administrators over the province of Babylon. In the meantime, Daniel actually served in the royal court (Daniel 2:48,49).

Daniel's testimony was so well-known that he must have been deliberately sent out of town on business during the event. In Daniel 3, where we read the story of his three friends and the furnace of fire. Daniel is nowhere to be found. This time his friends would have to take their own stand for God.

Halftime

1. *Am I really willing to stand up for my beliefs, or do I depend too much on my friends?*

2. *What stand should I be taking right now that I am hesitant about?*

Bend, Bow, or Burn!

Nebuchadnezzar was your typical autocratic egomaniac. Power corrupted him so thoroughly that he eventually lost his mind. He loved things that called attention to himself. So he eventually constructed a 90-foot gold statue of himself.

Then he invited all the provincial officials (except Daniel) to a public dedication of the statue.

"As soon as you hear the sound of the horn, flute, zither, lyre, harp, pipes, and all kinds of music," announced a herald, "you must fall down and worship the image of gold" (Daniel 3:5).

It was bad enough making his people worship all those Babylonian gods, but now the king was demanding that they worship him. Even worse, if you didn't do it you would be "thrown into a blazing furnace" (3:6).

Ancient Babylon was covered with brick kilns. These "blazing furnaces" were used to fire the bricks for massive construction projects. There was very little wood in Babylon, since it is in the desert, so bricks were used to build everything from houses to palaces to walls. Such furnaces typically were conical in shape with a door at the bottom and an opening at the top.

The band played and the people bowed. It was quite the ceremony. Nebuchadnezzar stood there smiling from ear to ear—that is, until the astrologers interrupted him and denounced the three Jews for not bowing down. They were probably still angry that he had promoted the Jews to positions of leadership. This was their chance to get them in trouble.

"Shadrach, Meshach, and Abednego . . . pay no attention to you, O king. They neither serve your gods nor worship the image of gold you have set up," the astrologers asserted (3:12).

Nebuchadnezzar blew up in a fit of rage! His big day had been spoiled by these stubborn Jews and jealous astrologers. He summoned Shadrach, Meshach and Abednego and demanded an explanation. Then he threatened them with execution.

"Then what god will be able to rescue you from my hand?" he insisted (3:15).

"O Nebuchadnezzar, we do not need to defend ourselves before you in this matter," the Hebrews responded. "If we are thrown into the blazing furnace, the God we serve is able to save us from it, and he will rescue us from your hand, O king. But even if he does not, we ... will not serve your gods or worship the image of gold" (3:16-18).

Standing at All Costs

Notice their response was twofold: 1) God is able to deliver us, 2) but He may not choose to deliver us. Either way, they were determined to stand up for their convictions. Now that is true courage! Humanly speaking, they had everything to gain by compromising. But spiritually speaking, they had everything to lose: their character, their integrity, and their commitment.

Nebuchadnezzar was furious! Their decision was pure defiance of his authority. He ordered the furnace to be heated seven times hotter than normal. That's the illogic of anger. The more intense heat would only kill them more quickly! But such decisions never make sense anyway. Nor did throwing them down through the opening in the top. Nevertheless, the king ordered it, so that's what they did. The soldiers climbed the ladder on the outer surface of the furnace and threw the three Jews into the blazing fire down below.

> *Humanly speaking, they had everything to gain by compromising. But spiritually speaking, they had everything to lose: their character, their integrity, and their commitment.*

Nebuchadnezzar peered into the furnace from the little window in the lower door and was shocked when he saw four people walking around in the fire unharmed.

"Look!" he shouted. "I see four men walking around in the fire...and the fourth is like a son of the gods" (Daniel 3:25).

Babylonian law codes always specified the concept of "trial by ordeal." In other words, if someone were thrown into a river—or a fire—as punishment and survived, they were presumed innocent.

It is no wonder then that Nebuchadnezzar ordered the Hebrews to come out of the furnace and exonerated them. They had survived the ordeal unharmed. Even the royal advisers had acknowledged the miracle.

"Praise be to the God of Shadrach, Meshach and Abednego, who has sent his angel and rescued his servants!" Nebuchadnezzar said. "They trusted in him...and were willing to give up their lives rather than serve or worship any god except their own God" (3:28).

> *When men are willing to die for what they believe, they will also be willing to live for what they believe.*

Two things jumped out at me from this account. First, it was an incredible testimony to Nebuchadnezzar. The pagan king was impressed by their courage and by God's power. Until you are willing to take such a stand, the power of God will never be evident in your life.

Second, the Hebrews put their fate in God's hands. They were willing to give up their lives for their beliefs. Some call this the "theology of martyrdom." Martyrs are those who are willing to die for their faith. When men are willing to die for what they believe, they will also be willing to live for what they believe.

The Fellowship of the Unashamed

Very few Americans ever face this option. Rarely are any of us called upon to die for our faith in Jesus Christ.

But until we are willing to die for Him, we will never fully live for Him. The true martyr is the one who believes his testimony is more important than his safety, and his faith more important than his life.

The following words of a martyred African Christian were found written on the walls of his prison cell:

> I am part of the Fellowship of the Unashamed. I have the Holy Spirit's power. The die has been cast. I have stepped over the line. The decision has been made. I am a disciple of Jesus Christ. I won't look up, let up, slow down, back away, or be still. My past is redeemed, my present makes sense, and my future is secure. I am finished and done with low living, sight walking, small planning, smooth knees, colorless dreams, tame visions, mundane talking, chintzy giving, and dwarfed goals.
>
> I no longer need pre-eminence, prosperity, position, promotions, plaudits, or popularity. I don't have to be right, first, tops, recognized, praised, regarded, or rewarded. I now live by presence, learn by faith, love by patience, lift by prayer, and labor by power. My pace is set, my gait is fact, my goal is heaven, my road is narrow, my way is rough, my companions few, my guide reliable, my mission clear.
>
> I cannot be bought, compromised, deterred, lured away, turned back, diluted, or delayed. I will not flinch in the face of sacrifice, hesitate in the presence of adversity, negotiate at the table of the enemy, ponder at the pool of popularity, or meander in the maze of mediocrity. I won't give up, back up, let up, or shut up until I've preached up, prayed up, stored up, and stayed up the cause of Christ.
>
> I am a disciple of Jesus Christ. I must go until Heaven returns, give until I drop, preach until all know, and work until He comes. And when He comes to get His own, He will have no problem recognizing me. My colors will be clear.

Enduring to the End

Daniel lived all the way through the 70 years of the Babylonian captivity. His courage as a young man paid off time and time again. He stood up against Nebuchadnezzar and eventually won him over to faith in his God. He stood against the king's wicked grandson Belshazzar and saw his kingdom fall to the Medes and Persians. Finally, he stood against Darius the Mede, the new ruler of Babylon who served under Cyrus the Great.

His last stand got him thrown in a lion's den when he was an old man of about 85. When ordered not to pray to anyone but the local king, Daniel continued praying to God three times a day with the windows open. He was a true servant of God, not some "secret agent" believer sleuthing around unidentified. He stuck out in a crowd because he was down on his knees talking to God.

Daniel's jealous critics rushed to Darius and accused Daniel of breaking the law because he prayed in public places. Some things never change! Satan is still trying to keep people from prayer. It is the one thing he fears most. When we are talking to God, we are in communication with the one and only Person who can overcome all opposition.

Daniel survived the "trial by ordeal." He lived through the night in the lion's den. "My God sent his angel, and he shut the mouths of the lions," Daniel called to the king. "They have not hurt me, because I was found innocent in his sight" (Daniel 6:22).

Daniel was released, and his accusers were given his punishment instead. The lions tore them to pieces. And Daniel was vindicated for his stand. In fact, Darius was so impressed, he issued the following decree:

> For he is the living God, and he endures forever; his kingdom will not be destroyed. His dominion will never end. He rescues and he saves; he performs signs and wonders in the heavens and on the earth. (Daniel 6:26,27).

Signs and wonders! That got the king's attention. Daniel's testimony made a lasting impact on everyone who knew him. Friends and enemies alike were overwhelmed by his courage and his faith. God moved powerfully on his behalf because Daniel stood up for his faith in Him.

Daniel was so beloved of God that the Lord unveiled the future to him through his many visions of the end times. He saw the Son of Man coming on the clouds of heaven and receiving a kingdom from God the Father, the "Ancient of Days." Daniel wrote: "His dominion is an everlasting dominion that will not pass away, and his kingdom is one that will never be destroyed" (Daniel 7:14).

Although it seemed bleak, the promise was not forgotten, nor was it in any serious jeopardy. The eternal God was still on the throne. The Promisor would maintain and fulfill the promise—just as He always had.

Postgame Highlights

1. What are you really living for in this life?

2. What are you willing to die for?

Personal Interview

How is God using your life and testimony to impact others?

Family

_____

_____

_____

_____

Friends

_____

_____

_____

_____

Relatives

_____

_____

_____

Acquaintances

_____

_____

_____

_____

Final Wrap-up

*If you don't stand up for something,
you will fall for everything!*

–Cal Thomas

Building for the Future:

Leaving a Legacy You Can Be Proud Of!

Men who really get somewhere in life build for the future. They begin with the end in view. Goals enable them to stay focused on where they are going and how they are going to get there.

Developmental psychologists tell us the final stages of life involve productivity and integrity. That is quite an admission from secularists who often tell us to indulge our passions and curiosity. But even they realize that when you get on with life, your life needs to become productive, satisfying, and fulfilling.

Selfish people don't think about the future. They expend everything in the present. When the future finally arrives, as it always does, they often find themselves in bitterness and despair. Living for today doesn't prepare us well for tomorrow.

Developmental stages in life are generally charted like this:

STAGE	QUALITY
Infancy	Trust
Childhood	Purpose
Adolescence	Identity
Early Adulthood	Intimacy
Middle Age	Productivity
Old Age	Integrity

When we get to the end of the line, we need to be on the right track. We ought to be able to look back over our lives with a sense of integrity. We need to feel that we did the best we could—we made right choices, corrected wrong choices, and left a positive legacy behind for our family and friends.

Men who really get somewhere in life build for the future

The idea of legacy-building is often discussed in books about older adults. The Southern Baptist churches have even formed a men's ministry called Legacy Builders. Most of us want to be remembered beyond our own time. We want to make a difference in our lifetime and leave something behind that we can be proud of: a solid marriage, a family estate, an inheritance for our children. But most of all, we need to leave behind a testimony of God's grace in our lives.

If we make the wrong decisions when we are young, we tend to set our lives on the wrong course. Once you're moving in the wrong direction, it is difficult to reverse yourself and turn around. God can intervene to help us, but we are often left with the regrets of wasted years.

A Simple Invitation

The sooner you get focused on where you are going, the better off you will be in the long run. Twenty-five years ago, I met a dynamic young businessman in Clearwater, Florida, named Herman Bailey. He had blond hair and blue eyes and dressed like a *Gentleman's Quarterly* model. You couldn't miss him if you tried! He made an immediate impression on everyone he met.

Herman was wrestling with making a commitment to full-time Christian service. I didn't realize it at the time, but he was also going through some very serious personal struggles. As these intensified, he began to think seriously about taking his own life.

In the meantime, we moved to Lynchburg, Virginia, where I began teaching at Liberty University. One morning, I stopped off at the local Howard Johnson's restaurant for breakfast and ran into Herman. He was sitting alone and seemed surprised to see me.

"Hey, what are you doing here in Lynchburg?" I asked.

"Oh, I just needed to get away," he said, "so I came up to check out a few things and get some things sorted out."

It wasn't unusual for people to just show up in Lynchburg in those days. In fact, it still isn't! It has long been a center of evangelical pilgrimage. People seemed to think if they just came there and saw Jerry Falwell, things would go better for them. It was one of those unique places where God was working in people's lives.

We talked through breakfast and reminisced about our time together in Florida. I never picked up on Herman's despair. He was always good at hiding his feelings behind his world-class smile. But I did sense that he needed a friend and that he was reaching out for something.

"Where are you staying?" I asked.

"At the motel next door," he responded.

"What are you doing for dinner?" I inquired.

"Nothing, really," he replied.

"Good! Then why don't you come over to our house for dinner tonight," I insisted.

"Are you sure?" he said.

"Donna doesn't mind," I assured him. "She always cooks for the family, and there will be plenty for you, too."

A Personal Turning Point

Herman agreed and came for dinner that night. Little did we realize that he had really come to town out of total desperation. He was actually planning to go back to Florida and commit suicide!

Years later, Herman told me that my simple invitation to dinner saved his life. Instead of driving home in despair, he refocused on coming over for dinner that night.

Sometimes the greatest legacy we can build is the lives of other people.

"As I watched your family, I realized I couldn't go through with it," he said. "You were playing with your children before dinner and I thought, 'I can't do this to my kids!' "

Herman Bailey went home to Florida and surrendered to full-time Christian ministry. He and his wife, Sharron, started the largest and most successful senior citizens' ministry in the whole country. They ministered to over 1000 seniors every week in the "Super Sixties" ministry at their church.

A few years later, Herman and Sharron were invited to start their own syndicated television show, "Action Sixties," on channel 22 in Clearwater. They have been on television five days a week for nearly 20 years, touching the lives of millions of people with a message of love and hope. All because of one simple invitation.

Sometimes the greatest legacy we can build is to touch the lives of other people. Every time God uses us to touch someone else, we are reaping dividends that have eternal significance. We are building a legacy of faith that can be transmitted from one generation to another.

Time Out

1. *Are you satisfied or dissatisfied with your life's work?*

2. *Are you having a positive influence on others?*

Hard Times for the Jews

Legacies can be built in many ways. Some are personal, some financial, and some are even national in scope. The nation of Israel is one such legacy. God promised them an everlasting inheritance. And throughout the centuries, God has raised up great men to keep His promises to them—and us—alive.

The story of Nehemiah's successful efforts to rebuild the walls of Jerusalem is a powerful account of legacy-building for the future. Some time after Daniel had been taken captive to Babylon in 605 B.C., the Jews rebelled against Nebuchadnezzar, and the Babylonian king destroyed Jerusalem and Solomon's Temple in reprisal in 586 B.C.

The "Babylonian Captivity," as it came to be known, lasted 70 years (605-535 B.C.). Babylon eventually fell to the Medes and Persians in 538 B.C. Cyrus the Great, the

Persian Emperor, decreed the Jews could return home in 535 B.C. About 40,000 made the difficult journey back to Jerusalem and Judea, which lay in ruins.

A man named Zerubbabel led the Jewish "remnant" to rebuild the Temple, which was completed in 515 B.C. It was a time of great renewal and revival among God's people. They were actually back in their homeland, and a Temple again stood on Mount Moriah. The promise again took hope for a better future. The line of the Messiah had been preserved. But not without difficulty.

The Jews were hated by their neighbors and misunderstood in general. Xerxes came to the throne in Persia and eventually married a Jewish girl named Esther. When a madman named Haman tried to get Xerxes to exterminate the Jews, Esther intervened, and her people were spared.

Later, Artaxerxes came to the Persian throne and authorized Ezra the scribe and a small number of Jews to return to Jerusalem in 458 B.C. When they arrived, they found things in great disarray. The Temple was still there, but there was great disregard for the Law of God or the things of God. What's worse, the city walls had never been rebuilt. The Jews were utterly defenseless against their enemies.

A Plan of Action

Nehemiah rode out at night to inspect the ruined walls and gates of the city. Upon his return, he gathered the Jewish leaders together and announced his intentions.

"You see the trouble we are in," he stated. "Jerusalem lies in ruins, and its gates have been burned with fire. Come, let us rebuild the wall of Jerusalem, and we will no longer be in disgrace" (Nehemiah 2:17).

Rebuild the walls! They had been in a state of ruin for three generations. It was a bold plan, and it captured their hearts.

"Let us start rebuilding," the leaders agreed.

And the work began. Even the priests got involved. Various people took responsibility for the different sections of the wall: Eliashib and the priests; men of Jericho; sons of Hassenaah; Meremoth son of Uriah; Meshullam son of Berekiah; Zadok son of Baana; men of Tekoa; Joiada son of Paseah; men of Gibeon and Mizpah; Uzziel, one of the goldsmiths; Hananiah, one of the perfume-makers; and many more.

Different men from different places with different gifts and abilities all contributed to the work. They worked as a team and got the job done in record time—52 days (Nehemiah 6:15). Nehemiah had proven to be just the leader they needed. He gave them:

1. Vision
2. Motivation
3. A plan of action

Halftime

1. Am I building a legacy for the future?

2. How can I motivate others to do the same?

The Power of Vision

Nehemiah saw a vision of a better future for Jerusalem. He realized the city had no future without walls. It was commendable that the Jews had rebuilt the Temple first. But they had left it standing defenseless without walls around the city. There can be little doubt that they discussed this matter. They probably talked about it constantly. But no one did anything about the problem.

It has often been observed that most organizations are underled and overmanaged. That was also the case with the Jews at Jerusalem. They remained busy about their daily tasks in the Temple without taking time to make it secure. Everyone knew the city needed walls, but nobody had the vision to get the job done.

Some have defined vision as foresight with insight based on hindsight. Vision includes these key components:

1. Realistic view of the present.
2. Optimistic view of the future.
3. Honest assessment of one's resources.
4. Positive attitude about change.
5. Specific plan of action.

Nehemiah's vision for a secure city kept him focused on his goal. Opposition from local detractors such as Sanballat, Tobiah, and Geshem did not deter him. With a sword in one hand and a mason's trowel in the other, Nehemiah led the rebuilding of the stone wall.

His enemies threatened to tell the Persian king that he was a traitor plotting a revolt. "We'll tell him people are saying, 'There is a King in Judah!'" they threatened.

Some have defined vision as foresight with insight based on hindsight.

But Nehemiah would not be frightened. After all, he knew the Persian king personally. The king knew that Nehemiah was an honest man. So the work proceeded on schedule. The people volunteered to work, gave offerings, and took collections to get the job done.

One man's vision stirred an entire nation to action. Jerusalem would once again be a viable city with a hope and future. And the promise would be kept alive for 400 more years.

Read the genealogy of Jesus Christ in Matthew 1:12 and you will discover Zerubbabel, the son of Shealtiel. This is the very man who led the Jews to return and rebuild the Temple 75 years before Nehemiah arrived to rebuild the walls of Jerusalem (cf. Ezra 5:2 and Haggai 2:23).

In the person of Zerubbabel, the messianic seed returned to the Promised Land. The stage was set again for the coming of the Messiah to fulfill the promise. And God used a man named Nehemiah to make the city secure for the arrival of her King.

Winning at Work

Nehemiah's leadership reflects the basic qualities of all great leaders. He saw a need and met it. He saw a problem and solved it. He saw the future and realized it. That is vision.

Success in any enterprise includes the basic elements of leadership:

1. *Commitment.* Nehemiah risked his position, reputation, and even his life to get the job done. When he arrived in Jerusalem, he spoke with such commitment that the people followed him gladly.

2. *Motivation.* He was able to motivate others to action. They got the job done because Nehemiah convinced them it was the will of God. Therefore, God would help them do the job.

3. *Teamwork.* Nehemiah knew he couldn't do the job alone. So he gathered an entire team of leaders, helpers, and servants. Together, they got the job done in record time. They all took a share of responsibility for the work load. And they all felt a shared fulfillment in a job well done.

4. *Decisions.* At every turn in the process, Nehemiah expressed decisiveness. He knew what needed to be done, so he made the decisions necessary to get it

done. He never hesitated or vacillated. He moved ahead, and the people moved with him.

5. *Goals.* Nehemiah refused to be deterred from his basic goal. He was determined to get the wall built. So he refused to be distracted by enemies and critics.

6. *Accomplishments.* Real leaders get a great deal of fulfillment from accomplishing their goals. They love the challenge of the task, the process of the work, and the rewards of a job well done.

7. *Celebration.* Great leaders celebrate the success of others. They are not jealous or envious of the success of others. They realize that we all share in each other's success. And that builds a greater team.

National Revival

When the work was finished, Nehemiah gathered the Israelites in a great national assembly in the square before the Water Gate (Nehemiah 8:1). He intended it to be a great national celebration for God's blessings on the people.

"Enjoy choice food and sweet drinks," he said. "Celebrate with great joy" (8:10,12).

Nehemiah understood the value of celebrating and commemorating their success. He wanted this time to go down in their history as a time of great blessing. "The joy of the LORD is your strength," he announced (8:10).

But when Ezra brought out the Book of the Law and read it at the assembly, the people began to weep and cry. They were convicted of their sins and repented before the Lord. As Ezra read the Law and praised God, the people shouted, "Amen! Amen!" Then they bowed down and worshiped the Lord (8:6).

After seven days of celebration, the people held a solemn assembly on the eighth day. The whole process was a celebration of the Feast of Tabernacles, which commemorated the exodus and their wilderness journey. Now, thanks to Nehemiah's leadership, they were celebrating a new return to the Promised Land.

On the last day of the feast, the Israelites assembled in sackcloth and separated themselves unto the Lord (9:1). They corporately confessed their sins as a nation and renewed their covenant with God, sealing the binding agreement with their names. People, priests, Levites, leaders, singers, gatekeepers, and Temple servants. They all signed it. And the nation of Judah was reborn.

The revival under Ezra and Nehemiah set the stage for the next 400 years. With Nehemiah's reforms and Malachi's final prophecy, the Old Testament canon of Scripture came to a close. Four hundred "silent years"

Our spiritual heritage today is based upon those Hebrew heroes who dared to believe God

would follow with no new revelation from God. The Old Testament closes, leaving us expecting the promise to be fulfilled in the future.

Malachi, the last prophet, wrote, " 'I will send my messenger, who will prepare the way before me. Then suddenly the Lord you are seeking will come to his temple; the messenger of the covenant, whom you desire, will come,' says the LORD Almighty" (Malachi 3:1).

The Promisor would not forget the promise. He would continue to keep it alive in the hearts of His people until it was time. Then, He would come–the Messiah, the One they desired all along. He would come in person and make good all the promises of God.

We are left standing on the Temple Mount peering into the distance as the Old Testament closes. We are looking down the corridor of time through the canyon of eternity.

There, on the horizon, we see a young man making His way from Nazareth to Jerusalem. He is going to the Temple with His disciples. He is on His way to keep the promise.

Our spiritual heritage today is based upon those Hebrew heroes who dared to believe God. Our spiritual journey began with those first steps of faith which they took down the long road of God's grace. They have left us a legacy that endures to this day. May we, by God's grace, leave a legacy to our children that will endure for generations to come as well.

Postgame Highlights

1. *Where do I need to improve as a leader?*

2. *What steps of action should I take to become a better leader?*

Personal Interview

What is my vision of the future for my life and family?

_____

_____

_____

_____

Final Wrap-up

What you leave behind will tell people what you were really all about.

—Ed Hindson

Epilogue:
Making a Difference

Life is a pilgrimage. It is a process of growth. And there are no shortcuts to maturity. You can only get there by walking the rough road of life, no matter what obstacles may lie in your way. But each step is a divinely appointed opportunity to bring us closer to the pinnacle of spiritual growth and maturity.

We can have confidence that as we walk in the road of life, we have in Christ the resources to face any problem that comes our way. We are in His love and care. We can look beyond the temporal and press on to the eternal. We need not be defeated by our failures; our victory has already been assured by Christ.

Whatever your problems may be, they pale into insignificance in the light of eternity. No matter how great your failures, God's grace is greater still. So lift up your heart and face life head-on. Don't avoid your problems; tackle each one directly, knowing that God will help you through. The tougher the problem, the greater His grace will be.

Remember, no one is totally successful all the time. When we are on top of things, we need to lift up those who are down, so that when we are down they can lift us up. That is what the family of God is all about. Each person ministers to another so that all are helped. Not only can we learn from our own mistakes, but we can share with others how we've overcome them. And we can be encouraged as others share their experiences with us.

Never give up! You can't win the race in the first lap. Life is a marathon, not a hundred-yard dash. The last hill always seems like the toughest. You have to keep running until you're finally home. Pace yourself. Be prepared for the detours and trouble spots. When they come along, don't give up the race. Remember, when the going gets tough, the tough get going.

God understands your struggle. He designed the trouble spots to toughen you and mature you for the final lap. He also knows how much you can take. He will never put more on you than He has put within you to meet the challenge.

When the race is run and your goal is reached, you will be able to say with the apostle Paul, "I have fought the good fight, I have finished the race, I have kept the faith." (2 Timothy 4:7).

In the meantime, run the race with the goal in view:

1. *Face Reality.* Admit your struggles and weaknesses. Don't pretend things are fine when they really need improvement. Denial may bring temporary relief, but never a permanent solution.

2. *Take Responsibility.* Deal with your own life. No one else can solve your problems for you. You must do that yourself with God's help. Confront your problems honestly and correct them.

3. *Do the Right Thing.* There is a right way and a wrong way to handle every situation in life. Find the right way to do it! God's Word will guide you into the truth.

Remember, we are "children of the promise" (Romans 9:8). We are the recipients of a great spiritual heritage. Other men of God have already paved the way for us. And that great "cloud of witnesses" (Hebrews 12:1) is standing in the bleachers of heaven cheering us on to victory.

The Promisor has given our entire generation the opportunity to live out His promises in our lifetime. In this book we have seen how we can benefit from the lessons of the past. But we must take the ball and run with it ourselves if we are going to make a difference in our families, businesses, churches, and communities.

The time has come for today's men to answer God's call on their lives. It is a time for courageous faith and masculine determination. A time to stand up for what we believe and claim this generation for God.

The Promisor is calling for men who will believe His promises. Men who will step out by faith and live for Him. Men who will place themselves in the hands of God. Men who will surrender themselves to His will and purpose for their lives.

Such men are *Men of the Promise.* They are not ordinary men. They are men of faith, commitment, and action. They are men who are willing to meet the challenges of life and stand victorious.

Will you be one of them?

Other Good Harvest House Reading

PROMISING WATERS
by *Jim Grassi*

Filled to the limit with anecdotes, humor, and adventure stories, *Promising Waters* will catch the attention of every man, outdoorsman or not, who wants to know more about walking with Jesus every day. National fishing instructor and television cohost Jim Grassi explores the parallels between fishing and discipleship, showing men how to create an atmosphere of openness, wisdom, and guidance that promotes deep relationships. Tim Hansel says, "One day Jim made the connection between his avid love for fishing and his even more avid love for Jesus Christ. Sparks began to fly!"

THE TOTAL CHRISTIAN GUY
by *Phil Callaway*

Come. Be brave. Venture into the mind of a Christian guy. Find out why he would rather pray than move furniture. Uncover his mysterious fascination with remote controls. In this collection of humorous stories, you'll meet regular Christian guys like Phil—guys who fall, but can get back up. Who can laugh in the face of the storm. Described as "Dave Barry with a message," Phil Callaway shows, amid the laughter, why real men have their eyes fixed on Jesus.

THE INTERNATIONAL INDUCTIVE STUDY BIBLE
New International Version
by *Precept Ministries*

Since the introduction of *The International Inductive Study Bible* with the New American Standard text, people have eagerly awaited the release of the NIV edition. Every feature of this unique study Bible is specifically designed to help young and old gain intimate understanding of God's Word. Unlike other study Bibles, it does not lead to a particular interpretation of the text but teaches readers to discern God's truth for themselves. Simple, easy-to-understand instructions for every book of the Bible lead men and women through the process of inductive study: observing what the text says, interpreting what it means, and applying the discovered truth personally.

NO GREATER SAVIOR
by *Richard Lee* and *Ed Hindson*

Nothing can compare to walking intimately with the Savior. Authors Lee and Hindson show how, in Jesus' presence, the weak became strong, the poor became rich, and despair turned to hope. *No Greater Savior* is an invitation to draw near to Jesus and be changed . . . forever.

THERE'S HOPE FOR THE HURTING
by *Richard Lee*

Using illustrations from everyday life as well as examples from the lives of Bible personalities, Dr. Lee reminds us that God will restore and redeem those who cry to Him "out of the depths."

GOD'S MAN IN THE FAMILY
by *Floyd McClung*

Unrealistic expectations and burdens have made it nearly impossible for today's Christian man to keep up with his role as husband and father. Discover the Bible's refreshingly short list.